THE
AUTHENTIC
WIFE

"She has but she doesn't possess,

Acts but doesn't expect.

When her work is done, she forgets it.

That is why it lasts forever."

-Lao Tzu, Tao Te Ching

THE AUTHENTIC WIFE

Uncaging Yourself Through Marriage

Beth Rowles

To My Beautiful Children:

May You Never Need This Book.

Table of Contents

Introduction 1

Chapter 1: *The Princess Effect* 5

    Authentic Action Step #1: 17

Chapter 2: *Glass Ceilings Fit for A Princess* 19

    Security 20

    Attraction 25

    Delusions & Discomfort 27

    A New Way 29

    Authentic Action Step #2: 32

Chapter 3: *A New Chapter Begins* 33

    The Anxiety of Perfection 34

    Conditioned Expectations 40

    Resentment 42

    Releasing Expectations 45

    Reacting 49

    The Loving Choice 50

    Pressure to Grow 54

    Authentic Action Step #3: 56

Chapter 4: *Love Starts in the Heart* 57

    True Love 58

    Fight or Flight 64

    Arguments 65

    Lack 66

    Receiving Love 68

    Self Worth 70

Abundance / Love 72

Self Care 73

Meeting Your Needs 76

Your priorities MUST be: 78

Getting Your Needs Met 79

Shift Up 80

Tune In 81

Turn the Dial Meditation 81

Turn the Dial Journaling 83

Authentic Action Step #4: 84

Chapter 5: *Invitation To The Crystal Ball* 85

Patterns 86

The Narcissist 88

Gaslighting 89

The Empath 91

Emotional Enmeshment 92

Enabling 95

Giving Myself Away 96

I Saw the Sign 100

Stop Doing It All 102

The Turmoil of Change 103

Emotions as Guidance 104

Boundaries 105

Trust 108

Intuition 109

Changing Patterns and Setting Boundaries 113

Authentic Action Step #5: 114

Chapter 6: *Mirror, Mirror, One and All* 115

    Pull the Thorns..116

    Co-Creation...118

    Identifying the Mirror...119

    Why Awakening is Easier with Our Children 125

    Life is Like a Funhouse 126

    Authentic Action Step #6: 129

Chapter 7: *Practical Matters*..131

    Authentically You 132

    Values and Environments 134

    Material Things...137

    Money 140

    Sex 140

    Kids 141

    Chores...142

    Bills...145

    Food..145

    Pets 146

    Authentic Action Step #7: 147

Chapter 8: *Pleasure*..149

    Addiction 149

    When They're Grumpy..152

    Love Yourself Through It..155

    Authentic Action Step #8: 158

Chapter 9: *You're Cheating Yourself*..159

    Lies and Deceit...160

    The Care and Keeping of a Relationship.............................161

Making Waves, Making Love 164

When It's Too Late 167

Authentic Action Step #9: 170

Chapter 10: *Irreconcilable Differences* 171

Divorce 171

When Divorce is an Option 178

Who Wants the Divorce? 179

What You Focus on Grows 181

Thank and Release 182

Communication 184

Conflict/Communication 188

Offering Empathy 189

To sum it all up: 192

Authentic Action Step #10: 192

Chapter 11: *There is No Fear in Happiness* 193

Looking for Evidence to Leave/Co-Creation 195

Feel Evidence of Love 196

Mirror of the Fear 196

Move Out of Fear 200

What You Focus on Grows 202

13 Steps to Begin Reconnecting 206

Authentic Action Step #11: 208

Chapter 12: *Your One True Love* 209

The Lifetime Commitment 210

The Spiritual Partnership 211

Authentic Action Step #12: 217

Acknowledgments 219

Appendix..221

    Key Questions Before Marriage: 221

References & Recommended Reading..225

The Memory of Love..229

Thank You!...231

Introduction

I remember the first time I wondered if I'd made a colossal mistake choosing my husband. It wasn't long after my first child was born, and I remember standing in the shower after a fight and sobbing, wondering how I could have been so stupid.

I really thought I had it together by the time we met, yet now I was subjecting my kids to this lapse of judgment I'd made even after swearing I never would. They were going to suffer for my choice.

That was the moment I sent our marriage into new territory: down the path to divorce. Every day, millions stop at this fork in the road of life and turn down that path, and most never make it out.

We made it out.

So far.

This book is about the lessons I learned along the way, the deep healing that had to take place, and the realization that my husband was going to be my biggest awakener. He was going to push me off the cliff of stagnancy into a free-fall toward authenticity.

As of today, we've weathered one mentally ill relative, four deaths, three job losses, one move, and the births of two children. If it hadn't been for the lessons I share in this book, our family would—without a doubt—be separated and suffering by this point.

I'm thankful every day that I took this journey at a relatively young age and that my children are going to be (hopefully) forever changed by it.

Here's to you and your journey: please know I'm now walking with you, and if I can finally understand what it means to love myself and let her shine, so can you.

Much love. You've got this.

XO,

Beth

A Word on Inclusion for my LGBTQ+ Readers:

I honor relationship in ALL of its forms; man and woman, man and man, woman and woman, and beyond… I originally started writing with the intent to keep the language all-inclusive. I have realized, however, that the only relationship I personally can speak to is that of man and woman. I believe these are universal lessons for all relationships, of all genders and ages, but have used my own experience as a guide, so you will mostly see language from my limited perspective as a straight, privileged white woman. Please take what resonates and leave the rest.

If you live with anyone that hurts you, please get to safety. It is not necessary to stay with someone that abuses you to learn these lessons.

National Domestic Violence Hotline:

1-800-799-7233

www.thehotline.org

.

Chapter 1: *The Princess Effect*

We're caught up in a delusion, my friends—including my 60 million fellow married Americans. We've all been tricked into believing marriage is something we have to partake in to be "good" people—after all, sex without marriage is just an express ticket to hell.

We've created a system where it's nearly impossible to live without another, where bills add up, and some things even cost more if you're single. We've all bought into the idea that we must FIND or arrive at happiness, that it's a place you get to when you're married in the suburbs with 2.5 kids. While the divorce rate has been falling since the 1980's, we're still signing contracts and reciting ancient vows with people we barely know like that somehow makes any sense. It doesn't, but we do it anyway because we just want to be loved, to belong, to finally be special to someone, and to create the loving AND functional family we never had.

I fell for it completely, even after watching my own parents' marriage wither and die after years of yelling and recurrent application of the silent treatment. It was my mom's second wedding, so I guess she fell for it twice—even though her own parents were also divorced. At that time in the 1970's, being divorced was still a disgrace. From what I understand, half the family stopped talking to each other, except to let her know they hoped she fell off her horse at her next barrel race. This was said to my mother—not to her mother, who was the one actually getting the divorce from her longtime verbally abusive, alcoholic, and unfaithful husband. From the stories I've heard, all I can wonder is how my grandma stayed with him as long as she did. I guess it was shameful to not be married (especially with my mom on the way), and it was shameful to leave one.

An older single woman was called a "spinster" or an "old maid." I played that card game. I watched the fairytale movies. I wanted to be swept off my feet by a handsome prince that would solve all my problems. All the worthy girls rode off into the sunset with a new husband. Life didn't begin until an heir to the throne saved you from your miserable existence. Women off enjoying their lives were just weird, or at least not at all role models I was aware of. Where was the movie about the princess, or even a peasant, kicking ass and enjoying her single life? The closest I got to that was Alice in Wonderland, and her friends weren't even real.

Yet even as the child of a bitter divorce, I still longed for that ring, the diamond, the sense of belonging it seemed to hold in its reflective facets. I obsessed about all of it; the size of the rock, the way it was cut, the kind of metal it was held in, where it came from, the brand name, and how it looked on my (possibly manly) finger... As soon as I was in a relationship, I'd pass by jewelry stores and wonder if he would buy me the ring today.... Would he buy it next month? Would he ever buy it? It was as though my entire sense of belonging was to be purchased in a mall jewelry store, just sitting in a glowing glass case in the center of the twinkling carpet. A crown to be pulled for the princess. Was I worthy enough of a diamond, like all the other girls—like all the prettier, skinny girls?

I obsessed about what I still needed to change to be good enough for a ring. Clearly I needed breast implants, a nose job, straighter hair, a tummy tuck, different feet entirely... I needed to have cooler hobbies or be more athletic, or way funnier. Every time a stunning new actress graced the silver screen, I spent the entire movie analyzing what must make her so desirable to men. Was there any hope for me?

Finally, in 2008, I met The One. Strangely enough, he seemed to love me just like I was. I had finally arrived at perfection! Just kidding, I was still chubby and had the wrong color hair. He mentioned once in passing (referring to me, even) that he liked girls who had blue eyes and dark hair, like him. So there my blonde highlights went as I played with box after box of dye, trying to find the perfect brunette color. *I better change to keep him, or he's going to wise up and find his Angelina Jolie.* This was my ridiculous thought process: improve yourself to make someone else happy.

Likewise, managing my weight has never been about me, either—I always hear someone else's voice urging me to diet. Ever since my family's comments about it when I was young, it's been something I had to transform to gain someone's approval, to be accepted. There's nothing quite like two overweight women shaming you for eating, while eating, followed by a *"There's no hope left for us, but you have a chance!"*

This wasn't all in my head, either. My first boyfriend was so incredibly charming that he told me he'd marry me AND buy breast implants for me if I lost 20lbs. I took that knowledge and *gained* weight. Love me at my heaviest or don't love me at all, jerk! I also left him, which may seem like I finally dared to find someone who reflected my worth, when in actuality I was just motivated by someone else who had expressed interest and didn't seem like such a jerk (side note: he was).

But, I digress. Back to the ring. I had a good chance with The One. Mine was to be his third engagement ring purchase, so he was well-practiced. My predecessors didn't work out, and from what I knew of them, it was clearly all their problem, and he was nothing but the fantastic catch I declared him to be—well, the online matching site, eHarmony, declared him to be. He was tall, handsome, funny, and insanely sweet. One day early on, he picked me up at the office for lunch for the first time. I walked outside and saw this statuesque, tan, gorgeous specimen filling out a black bomber jacket that reflected the sunshine and made it look like he was just glowing. His face lit up with the biggest smile I'd ever seen when his eyes found me at the door. My knees were so weak I could barely cross the parking lot. I climbed onto the back of his motorcycle giddy with excitement that this man was actually here for ME. The whole affair was made even better by the fact that everyone at the office had just watched me crash and burn in love with a co-worker. To go from that debacle to this GQ-esque model of a man was sweet revenge.

He was more than just good-looking. We had such familiarity from the start I kind of wondered if he was actually family or even REAL. After all the duds I'd dated, he seemed way too good to be true. *With this much happiness, getting married is the obvious next thing to do...* I decided soon after our third date.

We looked at rings together from that moment on. I assured my new boyfriend that I didn't mind if it even had a real diamond. "You can buy me a real diamond on our 10th anniversary," I told him. I just wanted a band around my finger that meant I'd never have to go through the nightmare of dating ever again. Now that I'd finally found the needle in the haystack, I didn't want some other female to take him from me, either. I wanted him to be only mine.

I derived much of my worth from that single piece of overpriced jewelry. It's ironic to me that I'm sitting down to write this book and just discovered last night that a diamond has fallen out of my ring. It's about the fifth time that's happened. My ring is lined with pavé set small diamonds, and they just keep popping out from the stress of daily life, much like the wrinkles that only appeared after we tied the knot.

The day my now-husband finally bought the ring, I was there. Actually, two versions of me were there, in the Glenbrook Mall: *Adult Me* was angry that he was going to be adding to his debt, but something else in me was SO MESMERIZED by that rock and what it meant that I didn't object TOO strongly. Ah, such a precursor to what was yet to come. I was in another jewelry store looking at the ring I really liked when he financed this one. This was my second choice.

As he came to retrieve me, he saw his first fiancée strolling through the mall with her boyfriend, and abandoned me to go chat with her. Confident that she was bat-shit-crazy and therefore not a threat, I casually seized the opportunity to admire the ring *I* loved—a tension set princess cut—some more before I had to go see the one *he* really wanted. I didn't trust my taste, and it seemed at times like his was better. The truth was, I didn't yet trust myself. *The truth is also that the ring he picked is gorgeous.*

The sales lady looked at me incredulously, as if to say, "Are you nuts?!" when I told her why he disappeared so quickly. I was. We all are, my friends. He returned in a few minutes, and I followed him back to the other store to retrieve the small navy bag and walked, dazed, back out into the bustling mall. Then he completed the magical affair by saying, "So, are you going to wear it?" when we were standing in front of Auntie Anne's Pretzel Shop.

"You have to ask me."

"I don't ask dumb questions."

Oh, the shattered dreams of a fairytale proposal! I don't think he stopped walking. He may have gotten it out of the bag, but I don't even recall if he put it on my finger or not. Since it was his third time proposing perhaps he was just a little tired from that long movement down to one knee (he is 6' 7", after all), and didn't want to exert too much energy.

Looking back now, I see where my husband was foreshadowing what was to come. In his own lazy way, he was letting me know that this wasn't about theater. This wasn't about a fairytale. This wasn't about expectations. This was about walking together through life and life is definitely no fairytale. If I was going to accept this proposal, he knew I must be willing to accept him without expectation.

He knew that this ring didn't change who I was. He knew, maybe only subconsciously, that it meant very little. It was a want. It was a pretty piece of jewelry. It wasn't a symbol of his undying love, it was a $3,500 symbol of his willingness to make me happy.

Outside the mall, I sent a quick email to my folks then told everyone else that mattered via Facebook before we even pulled out of the parking lot. That was kind of the whole point of the ring, right? To declare ownership to the world? I can't even believe I'm typing those words now. In so many ways, I DID want to be "owned," and I definitely wanted to "own" him.

I wanted what the Disney movies promised. I wanted to be swept off my feet by a tall, dark, and handsome man (check) who would make me feel incredibly worthy by picking me over all of the other girls (check). I would then become something amazing…. A Wife.

At home, I immediately launched into wedding planning mode. When would we get married? Where would we get married? What would our colors be? What would my dress look like? Who would be in my wedding party?

Then, the shock and awe of this business that is weddings and the fact that he was indeed not a wealthy prince smacked me in the budget. *I'm sorry, did you say it would be $28 a PERSON for chicken?! Oh, just $15,000 to use this space for two hours? That dress is $6,900? Centerpieces are HOW MUCH?!?*

I just wanted to have a fun party with our friends. I wanted it to be outside, I wanted it to be warm, I wanted to have all of this beautiful symbolism about going on a journey and traveling together. I wanted to have a giant globe, and our colors were to be emerald green and peacock teal. I wanted to dance into the night, wrapped in a warm sea breeze.

We lived in the Midwest and he hates the beach.

No matter though, because our bank account had other ideas. When I realized what kind of party we could afford to throw, my heart sank in disappointment. I decided I wanted it to be beautiful or skip it entirely. With no help from our families (which we did not expect), we had two choices: don't do it or go into some significant debt. I was still recovering my credit score from all of the previous men I'd racked up debt for. He wasn't too far ahead of me on the debt front, and both of us lived paycheck to paycheck.

Finally, and much to his utter delight, I decided we'd just throw it all out the window and get married in the courthouse, followed by a lovely meal at my favorite wing place. *We'll do a destination vow renewal on our 5th anniversary*, I decided. *We'll have money then.*

When the big day finally came three weeks later, my dreams of at least being in a gorgeous marble and dark wood courtroom were abruptly ended when we were led to what was nothing more than a gray conference room with tables. The air was heavy with lingering emotions I could feel were not attributed to holy matrimony. I knew so little about what was going on that I didn't even want to stand on the left side during our vows. That seemed utterly wrong, but I shuffled over to the left when he insisted. I had no idea what to do or say, but I saw the love in his eyes as he teared up during the vows. The judge declared us husband and wife and my precious father-in-law said "Cha-ching."

My mother treated us, and the motley crew that showed up, to chicken wings and curly fries at my favorite place, Buffalo Wings & Ribs in Fort Wayne, Indiana. Enchanting. We watched the sun set on our fairytale day at the Melting Pot and swam in the pool at the Embassy Suites in Indy, where we spent the night. We both enjoyed the complimentary champagne before passing out for the evening—romance is not his forte.

The next morning, I'd arranged a ride for him on his one true love: a Ducati motorcycle. I waited patiently while he basked in the odiferous glow of an Italian desmodromic valve. Then we arrived home to the confusion of locked doors, and just as his fear was about to explode in anger, he found a key and burst through the door to find the house was filled with all of his closest friends, including his twin best friends for the past 32 years from Ohio. I'd arranged a surprise party, as we got married on his 35th birthday, and had hired a friend to decorate the house and set out all of the food I'd prepared before letting the guests in.

Honestly, not much about my "wedding" was about me. I was still firmly planted in worthless soil. At 25, I'd dated enough by the time I met my husband that I really thought I knew what I was doing. We were on the same page when we met. We were in the same paragraph in the same line, even. We talked about Maslow's characteristics of self-actualization! I really thought we touched on all the big things everyone says to discuss before you get married. Who cared that his father hated me and my mom was already less than thrilled about him—we knew what we were doing. Hell, we took that as a good sign! Little did we know that those were warning signs—but not in the way you might think. More on that later.

I felt like I learned so much by the end of each relationship that I was making the right choice. And I did. I attracted a man who was at my level of consciousness, if not a bit more in some areas. That's all we can hope for. We attract what we are.

The first few days as husband and wife were tense. We'd taken time off work, but we really didn't think we could afford to go anywhere. Finally, after much argument and debate, we decided to go somewhere close. We packed our bags and set out on his Goldwing, something I loathed doing already by that point.

Like every motorcycle trip we took, it was raining on our way down through the flat gloom of Ohio. I fumed inside, daydreaming about stretching out my legs in the car and not having to wear layers of waterproof clothing. I hated it! He'd bought this little black trailer by that point that we pulled with us, so I could actually bring my 60lbs of luggage. I tried so hard to be a good sport. Looking back (I haven't ridden since my first pregnancy,) I realize what a great bonding experience these trips on the bike were in the end. It really felt like we survived something by the time I pulled my stiff legs off and put them back on solid ground, for the crazy weather and conditions we would inevitably encounter along the way.

After a very long day of riding, we finally neared the mountains and pulled into the higher elevation of the Park Vista hotel in Gatlinburg, Tennessee. We enjoyed walking the town, Kilwin's chocolate, and the fresh mountain air. Every time I smell honeysuckle in bloom, I'm blessed with memories of our honeymoon.

After two nights exploring the twisty roads around Gatlinburg, and almost dying only twice, we rode over to Asheville and stayed at Biltmore (where I felt super judged for my helmet hair). The next day we climbed Chimney Rock which I hadn't done since I was a child, and finally ended our journey in Lake Lure, at the little motel where the actors in Dirty Dancing stayed while filming nearby. No Patrick Swayze fantasies were acted out, that's for sure.

It was rainy and dreary again as we pulled out of town, and we'd already had our fair share of little arguments. See, travel is like getting a full dose of life all at once. Life is consistently messy and unpredictable, we just try to control it and play it safe, so it doesn't seem this way. Only during travel do we seem willing to accept whatever comes up. You'll have flat tires and storms, be exhausted from hauling around your luggage and elated at the mystery of it all at once. Little did I know that this trip was such an excellent metaphor for what we'd just embarked on.

Like so many other women, I was thinking of the marriage only in terms of the destination, as if it was a place I was going, like a tourist. It was a happy place and would be fun and relaxed and exciting because everything would always be new, but he would stay the same. I would have a hot date, I would drink fancy drinks, we would both be smiling and loving every second of it and have sex whenever we wanted. He and I would be the unchanging constant, and we would take on life together. And perhaps more importantly, I would finally get the children I'd been longing for seemingly all of my life. I would finally get the love and approval I'd spent 28 years unable to find.

What I didn't realize, is that marriage is just the start of a personal journey; a traumatic trek not so unlike that of Frodo Baggins. It all starts with a ring, doesn't it?

I was about to travel to places that would test me, frighten me, and DEMAND that I find the courage to grow. It wasn't the actual circumstances of life that were the challenge. I'd already lived enough to know I could face and overcome those (or so I thought). It was HIM. It was ME. The bravery required to face oneself in the relationship mirror seems at times unobtainable, inconceivable, gigantic, and light years away. Leaving the comfort of what we know, the old familiar home—even with its toxicity and infestations, outdated appliances and leaking ceilings—

seems far more daunting than the discovery of the paradise that may be waiting upon landing.

WE were the uncontrollable variant. I didn't become some brand new and improved version just by marrying him. I carried every wound—every vulnerable, scared, disconnected, sad, yearning, hurting part—along with me, just like he did. The ring alone didn't freeze me in time.

I was going to continue to grow and change and, like visiting a new city where we don't know the language, I was going to be unfamiliar to him at times. He was going to do the same. We were going to have to explore each city and learn new languages continually on this journey, as life shifted beneath our feet and was new every moment. I would have to regain the awe I lost along the way.

Just like our body is completely brand new every seven years, due to cell death and birth (except the original eight cells called the "egg of life"), our life journey is full of new incarnations of us. Just think about who you were as a baby—clearly you are not that same person now. Who were you in high school? Who were you at 21? Who were you yesterday? We spend most of our lives thinking we have to carry that story—and old versions of us—with us. That is not the case, yet we do bring those buried beliefs we embedded into our psyche along the way, and relationship uncovers them like nothing else. Which we don't like either.

As we journey through this school called life, we evolve, we change, we grow, we metamorphize. That is why we come here. It is not to be successful or to cure cancer, though those are lovely results of what I'm talking about: it is to assist our soul in its evolution toward wholeness.

Every aspect of our lives is here for our own personal growth. I believe part of it is to accept responsibility for any unconscious choices we've made in this and other lifetimes and live in a new way where we don't hurt others. And part of it is to realize where others have destroyed us and imposed their limits and to have the bravado to say no more, to recognize that we are without limits.

So how can we choose, live with, and then sign a contract to never leave someone we may one day feel like we know nothing about? Someone who, through our own awakening, becomes unfamiliar or even unacceptable?

Four years after saying "I do" in the courthouse, I was recovering from the birth of our first child and drowning in responsibility. I started to wonder if I'd made a huge mistake. I felt like the rug had been pulled out from underneath me. This wasn't a happy place. This baby, who was a gift of pure love, didn't suddenly make this a happy place. In fact, it was like she came with the gift of a brand-new set of eyes for me.

I could suddenly see every perceived fault in my husband. I could suddenly detect every area where I wasn't getting what I wanted or needed. I could suddenly recognize where he seemed selfish or unkind or even unstable. She brought with her a removal of every filter we'd had in place that made our marriage seem like an unchanging tourist destination, a secluded all-inclusive resort of leisure and control.

She revealed every crack in our system. She uncovered every unhealed wound, every mismatch in values—every buried fear rose to the surface. It was one thing when the man I married didn't treat me well, but it was as though he detonated a bomb within when he didn't treat her well. Unable to see past my own misery, I laser-focused on his every "wrong" move and locked myself behind the rising walls of victimhood, where each exhausting day cemented me in further with each grievance the rebar at its core.

From a young age, I was shown I wasn't worthy in all the same ways as much of the rest of the world's children. It was a story I believed and tolerated. But from the core of my very being, I knew my child's worth and ANYTHING I perceived as behavior that didn't reflect that pricelessness opened up a volatile geyser of anger in my body.

Emotions are just energy in motion that we either allow to move out or shove down, storing it in the fascia of our body, like a cage. For three years after my daughter was born, that anger grew inside me until I was unrecognizable. I was kind and loving to my daughter and son and then cold and closed to my husband. The constant up and down was exhausting. I was always on alert, always protecting, and always wondering when he would cross the line and I'd have to leave.

Finally, I wanted out. I considered what had previously been unthinkable. Divorce officially became an option.

Authentic Action Step #1:

Identify the real why that's behind the reason why you got married.
What were you looking to soothe, heal, protect, or prevent?

Chapter 2: *Glass Ceilings Fit for A Princess*

To really shift into a new belief about relationships, we're going to have to journey through history a bit to understand how we ended up here.

Marriage itself is firmly rooted in fear and need of security, created initially to form alliances and control the ownership of property and power. Laws were created that encouraged reproduction, afforded citizenship, divided property, and usually maintained the male's power (either the bride's father or her husband) in all cases.

That sought-after diamond engagement ring and surprise proposal I dreamed about? They are also part of conditioning stealthily created by the De Beers diamond company around 1939, who started advertising and sentimentalizing this practice and ended up making it commonplace in our culture. And while the gold in your ring is an investment, a diamond is not, and most diamonds today are practically worthless.

The way marriage looks has changed, from polygamy to arranged child marriages to marriages within the family between cousins. While some cultures, like the Native Americans, saw no problem with homosexual marriage, in other cultures it didn't fit into the end goal of producing able-bodied citizens and controlling external power. It wasn't until about fifty years ago that we even included the ideas of equality, love, or mutual attraction in the marriage dialogue.

Even the vows that we recite are ancient, written at least 500 years ago but originating even earlier in medieval Catholic rites. We've been having and holding for a long time.

And look at these definitions of our coveted titles from Gary Zukav's *The Seat of The Soul.* Does this sound like what you signed up for?

Husband:

Male head of the household, from the Old Norse *húsbóndi* 'master of a house,' from *hús* 'house' + *bóndi* 'occupier and tiller of the soil.'

Wife:

Woman of humble rank, joined to man, hostess of the household

Matrimony:

Wedlocked mother, from Latin matrimonium 'wedlock, marriage,' from matrem (nominative mater) 'mother' + -monium, suffix signifying 'action, state, condition.'

I sure didn't think in terms of rank when I got married! And this idea of a "master of the house" probably makes you as ill as it does me. I don't know any woman today that wants a man to have control over her. And we're finally realizing how futile it is to try to have control over anyone other than ourselves.

Security

In all cases, marriage was intended for the survival of the species. Even today, we write our laws and develop systems that make it far easier to survive as a married couple. Combining assets gives us greater power, lowers the cost of insurance, and allows us to have more spending capacity as our level of disposable income increases. In the eyes of the law, only marriage even legitimizes our own children!

When I was single, I was making just enough to cover my most basic bills. I had to maintain the home on my own, figure out how to take care of my vehicles, mow the grass, shovel snow—all of the tasks of daily life. Should I become ill, there was no one designated to care for me outside of my parents who lived hundreds of miles away.

If my boyfriend were to be significantly injured in a motorcycle accident, I would have zero say in his medical care. This became a considerable pressure for me in our relationship. His bi-polar, paranoid schizophrenic relative could even deny my visits at the hospital and shut me entirely out of his life.

Having just extricated myself from a situation with a man who did have a severe accident which left him in a coma for weeks (putting a cramp in his philandering ways, I later discovered), I was well aware of the implications of not having any legal standing in this man's life just through the simple fact that I had no right to even visit him in the hospital. It's not uncommon to read horror stories about LGBTQ+ couples who are pushed out of their hospitalized long-term partner's life by unconscious and un-loving—even estranged—family members.

I knew that, waiting in the wings, was a mentally ill relative that had already declared me as unfit to be any part of his loved one's future. He made his desires to move in with my boyfriend and have him at his disposal repeatedly heard, demanding then begging that my future husband just leave his job to be his travel and bar buddy. My chances of him suddenly relinquishing his would-be new-found control were nil.

Though we both paid for our household bills (we moved in together quickly), I would have no legal say in claiming any of it if the unthinkable were to happen to him. I could be rendered homeless, at least temporarily, in less than a minute. I had sold my home by that point, and we had completely merged our lives.

I knew that marriage meant protection of my assets as well as what I perceived as control in our health and well-being. I knew that to be safe in this living arrangement, I needed some form of legal agreement. Having close to ten years of dating experience, I was well aware that relationships fail, anger boils, and one or both sides can ruthlessly attack out of bitter resentment. The only remedy I was aware of was marriage, though I imagine other contracts or arrangements exist.

I also knew that, should we end the marriage, we would be dividing assets. My husband's relative threatened him and tried to insist that I sign a prenuptial agreement, somehow deciding that by loving my husband and being attracted to him, I was actually declaring my want of the relative's money—just another symptom of the paranoid schizophrenia. A hilarious notion considering the fact that my entire life I'd given away money the moment it was received, hence my financial situation.

So, at the advice of someone older and wiser, instead of resisting this request, I called a lawyer and set up an appointment to have my own prenup written. Once I shared this with my fiancé, the matter was immediately dropped and on went the show!

When we sign up for this ancient archetype of marriage, we enter it at that level of consciousness: a financial arrangement predicated on lack and scarcity where the male is head of the house, and the female is a low-rank baby portal and humble servant to the male.

No part of this arrangement discusses our evolution or our spiritual path, or even our equality. For the majority of first marriages, and even most subsequent marriages, neither party likely even understands the ramifications of such a union. It is certainly not revered as a sacred partnership where each will undergo a transformation and support each other in growing, being non-possessive if they should actually grow apart.

In fact, I think most young adults believe that the marriage is a contract that will somehow stunt our non-physical growth and prevent change. After all, if someone grows, couldn't we grow apart? What if they evolve and leave us in the dirt? We sign the license with the intention to possess the other, seemingly oblivious to the individual paths we remain on despite the legal jargon.

To that end, marriage does control us into commitment. It is hard to leave a marriage, financially of course, but even just separating all of the assets, finding a new home, living on your own, putting the kids through the turmoil of it—it is monumentally challenging to do—especially after cohabiting for several years.

Not only that, we are hardwired to dislike change. We see change through a narrow lens of fear and uncertainty. We are terrified to walk through the exit door of what we know into what we don't. Yet that is what life begs of us to do! To be comfortable, our brains try to label and control every aspect of life, though life itself is just a series of unknowns and challenges.

We get married today with less knowledge of the terms and conditions of that contract than we have of our latest Apple iOS upgrade. We think name change, joint bank accounts, baby, happily ever after. We don't even stop to consider who the man or woman we're looking at might be in ten, twenty, or even just five years. Sure, we consider changes due to external events - *"Will you still love me if I'm in an accident and paralyzed from the waist down?"* But we don't consider even for a moment the possibility of our loved one to ever become unfamiliar internally.

Then the children come, and you realize you're now the managing partners of a very complicated household. Would you hire this person if your household were a business? Could you rely on them to pull their weight? Can you even have a productive conversation with them where you both agree on a solution? Can you even make a request of them and have it met?

We no longer live with extended family to help with childcare, finances, and housework—we insist on doing this all on our own, sometimes as far away from our families as possible. Can you really work full time, raise children, and care for your home? How will those tasks be divided? Where does nurturing the relationship itself fit in if you are so busy doing everything else?

And the most tragic part of all is that we marry with our heads and not our hearts. We use contrast to decide if they're a match: *Welp, he's better than the last asshole and has a stable job.* We left-brain-logic our way to the perfect partner. We have lists and checkboxes and physical requirements and rarely do we even have the capacity by that point to understand, honor, or even FEEL our feelings and intuition.

We don't even consider for a moment the possibility that a struggling relationship may not be what we call a "vibrational match." If we're at opposite ends of the spectrum, the relationship is passionate and we feel like the princess, until they realize we want to have a life too or we realize they are watching our every move. The question of where a potential partner is at in their spiritual evolution into consciousness isn't even in our vocabulary. We are solely focused on our needs being met by the other.

For many women, we never consider the possibility that we may transform, but we often marry with the presumption that we'll be able to change, even save, the man we're with. We see them as beings with potential who we can carefully craft into the perfect partner. We consider improving them, but we fail to view them as already capable of doing everything they need to do in their own life. We think our love will be enough. We are fully prepared to enable them to death. With this mindset, we look past the warning signs, we allow our seeming bleeding hearts to blind us, and we move forward with men who are just not our match.

Attraction

Biologically, as women, we're motivated by physical features that indicate the man's ability to protect us or provide for us. We may be instantly turned on by men who are tall, with big muscles and broad shoulders. All of us are drawn to mates who seem to have high procreation potential, even if children aren't yet on our radar. Some men are naturally attracted to women with wider hips or larger breasts, perceiving these as biological advantages for child rearing.

What we're physically attracted to as a culture changes based on what is the hardest to obtain in our time—in this day and age, a fit, tan body is the ideal. In previous times, overweight and pale was all the rage, because that meant you were able to sit inside and not labor. Skinny meant you were poor. Missed that boat, didn't we?

During this stage of attraction, our bodies are seeking out mates through a biological process using pheromones as well. We're literally breathing them in to decide if it's going to work, sniffing them out, even discerning whether or not we're RELATED.

Our brains are sizing up each suitor based on all of the subconscious conditions we've developed, primarily during the first six years of our lives. Author John Money calls this our "Love Map."

For men, their potential mate has to make them feel a certain way. She will fit into their idea of what a wife does for their husband. If they were raised in a home where mom did all of the housework and made the meals, then they have sought a woman that also appears to be capable of this. If they were neglected by their mother, they will likely be all about sex, and at first that may be flattering and fun.

Last night I asked my husband what surprised him most about our marriage. He said it was that I was able to do all of the things well that he struggled with. He literally, subconsciously, married me because of his survival instincts. He knew he needed someone who could make sure the laundry was done, who would keep food in the house, who would pay the bills and take care of the day-to-day minutiae because those were all areas that were not developed in his childhood and adolescence.

Some men are drawn to women who build up their confidence and erase their insecurities. And some men are so lost in their swirling ego that the woman is only to prop them up further in the eyes of others.

Likewise, each woman or partner is drawn to a man who fills her inadequacies.

But ultimately, real attraction comes from loving the way the person sees us. We actually like people the most when they reflect to us the best version of ourselves. This is also why we fear change—it rocks our sense of "enoughness" and threatens our very identity when we can no longer see ourselves in our spouse-mirror.

During the early stages of attraction, chemicals are firing and our minds are tricked into this euphoric state of bliss, where the other can do no wrong. Our egos make sure that we put forward the best version of ourselves needed to secure the partner it needs, leaving out the juicy detail that this role we're playing is going to disappear as soon as it feels satisfied that they're not going anywhere.

If we make it all the way to the wedding planning while still in this stage, we've done ourselves a great injustice. We've not allowed ourselves to move into a state of real love, which is a choice we make and not a result of their personality. Real love is not dependent on them at all. It is an internal state.

When we initiate the marriage thinking only about how our partner is going to make us feel, and not considering the potential for growth and development, we are then blindsided when they, and we, inevitably start to change.

When life activates our old wounds, and our patterns become too costly to ignore, we begin to look outward for someone to blame. Most of us, by this point, are still unaware of our own power to consciously create our lives. We see ourselves at life's mercy, not at the wheel in the driver's seat.

Delusions & Discomfort

We enter the contract of marriage based on survival, not based on a partner for our evolution. We are declaring a want for life to stay as is; comfortable, predictable, and secure. We choose to be with each other under the agreement that we'll always be like these happy, in-love people that we currently are. We don't think about months of depression, changes due to grief or anxiety from life's inevitable changes, or them being grumpy non-stop.

We shamelessly walk down the aisle of the institution of religion, put on jewelry declaring our entry into the institution of marriage, and utterly forget that we are divinity incarnate on a journey through the greatest school there ever was.

This made up thing we call marriage makes us believe we are owned. Possessed. You belong to me and I to you. We are wedLOCKED together. Though our nature is to explore sexually (especially for most men), the church tells us sex is a sin, and we are shameful if we do it and are not married, do it but not with the person we married, or if we have children outside of this legal partnership.

This delusion was created as a means to control, and we have completely fallen for it. I consider myself a strong, independent woman, and even I fell prey to this trap, so conditioned by society and the forms, or structures, we have set up that I was certain I needed to be married to be worthy.

And the most profound tragedy of all, we are convinced that we must always appear to be happy. While the tide is shifting to parents that are more emotionally intelligent, there is palpable discomfort in older generations when there is pain, such as when a toddler tantrums. Just the night before last when we were out to eat, my almost two-year-old had a very normal response to not understanding why he couldn't have the candy behind the counter, and an older man came over to distract him from his pain. We have been taught that discomfort is shameful and urgently must be transformed into something more acceptable.

Often, what is really happening is we are denying our own empathic abilities—our own gifts of feeling what another is feeling—because we don't know what's taking place and we've been taught it's better to avoid emotional pain at all costs rather than sit with it. Then the babies come with all of their raw emotions and women often find their husbands completely unwilling to "tolerate it," while they are struggling themselves as well.

So with this avoidance of any discomfort, of course, divorce is a shameful failure. Discord must mean one of us is bad. Fighting and disagreements are abnormal. Though the very nature of the marriage we buy into breeds jealousy and insecurity, we are admonished for being either.

In its traditional form, marriage is an impossible contract where we must both evolve at the same rate and be responsible for meeting every last need of our partner, and stay with them no matter how they treat us. It is entirely no wonder that marriages fail. From the very start, we have unreasonable expectations; for ourselves, our spouse, and our relationship.

A New Way

So that brings us back to marriage itself. If you are entering the consciousness of the man being the *master of the household* and the woman being the *humble servant and baby maker*, then do you think you will meet your intention of being equal powers? Of being loved equally?

If you look at wisdom leaders today, they often say they are in a "spiritual partnership." This means they have not entered the consciousness of "marriage," but the intention of an equal partnership in which both parties help each other evolve. There is no expectation other than standing in your truth and allowing the other to hold you accountable for growth.

Relationships are necessary for our spiritual evolution. Without them, we would almost never be pushed to grow. What a beautiful opportunity, therefore, to find someone you love who you want to walk through this lifetime with, to grow alongside! What a sacred opportunity, for two souls to hold hands through this life school, if only for a while.

This is not about the ring, the house, the chores... All of that isn't real. This is about our existence in virtual reality—the untouchable reality—the energy of our souls, our thoughts, our emotions... the energy of us! What do we have to walk through to allow that truth of who we are to shine through?

This is when your husband doesn't see your body as repulsive because you've gained weight, but as a sign that there is a pain you are trying to avoid through overeating. This is when your wife doesn't see your video game addiction as a flaw but as a sign that your reality is too much for you to be present in at the moment. This is when you both can look at chores as the adult responsibilities of this form-based life—and eventually as acts of self-love—and find a way together to make them manageable so neither is too heavily burdened by their weight. This is when you both look at money with respect, as abundant and plentiful when you are in your truth and giving value to the world, aligned to your purpose. This is when, if you do have kids, you see them as your great awakeners, great teachers of perfect presence and unconditional love. You view your sacred task of ushering them into adulthood with great reverence and put tremendous focus on not passing your own wounds down to them.

This is a beautiful place to be. This is more than the word marriage or even partnership could ever encompass. This is the flight of the soul.

It is so beautiful that it brings tears to my eyes to think about it. You are traveling through space in your physical body, being guided to wholeness by other souls you probably made arrangements to work with before you even incarnated. Not only are people here in the physical world helping to guide and awaken you to your highest potential, but you also have non-physical guides helping you as well. Do you know how supported you are? You are never alone. This is the whole point of your life. Every face you see in a crowd is a mirror, reflecting the most evolved parts of you or the parts still needing love and attention. Your spouse is the constant, inescapable mirror, either reminding you of your worth or reflecting your misbelief about it.

Take an honest look at your histories and the dynamics at play together. Discuss your childhoods, the way you were raised, the way your parents handled conflict, how they handled money, how they raised you, etc. These stories are a look at history so you can move forward with the intention to not repeat it, and with the awareness that these very same issues, coping skills, and behaviors will arise at some point in your relationship.

If you are committed to each other, you must be committed to your own personal growth as well as theirs. You must also be non-attached enough that you are ready to move on if that's what your growth leads to. We'll talk more about this later, but have the awareness that sometimes a partner may get stuck, or the relationship may no longer serve you in your growth. Sometimes the wounds will be too deep or the addictions too ingrained, or the conditioning too powerful. Sometimes you may just have very basic mismatches in your desires. As you step into your truth, what you want to do with your life may change dramatically. Just like your outer purpose changes throughout your life, your relationships may change with it.

Don't bury your head in the sand and avoid this truth of your evolution. Just like you have grown and changed throughout your life up to this point, you both will continue to do so. This is why marriage is an impossible contract. Unless you've taken a long look into the mirror, you have no idea what you are signing up for, and all you can control is your own role in the matter.

Heal your own wounds through the relationship and allow your partner to be the catalyst for immeasurable growth and spiritual evolution. Remember that they are not your clay to sculpt, but your mirror to reflect in. They are your beta tester. They are your most useful tool. This is not about owning or being owned, finding happiness or having your needs met. This is about the energy of love on our planet being exponentially increased by your willingness to look within and rise from the ashes of your past to the soaring heights of an untethered future.

Authentic Action Step #2:

To leave the cage, we must acknowledge it exists only in our minds. Now it is time to begin detaching from the conditioning our parents and culture created. Imagine that all you are attached to is already lost. If the "marriage" doesn't exist, what does the soul you live with (your partner) mean to you?

If so inspired, remove your wedding ring for a few days or a week. What do you experience? What reaction, if any, did they have?

Chapter 3: *A New Chapter Begins*

The labor for my first child was anything but magical. She was a week late, and my midwife insisted I be induced. We rolled in as happy as we could be Tuesday, but by the time she arrived at 3:30 AM on Thursday, I was starving and hadn't slept a wink since we walked through the doors. When we were finally released from their torture chamber Saturday, the new dad insisted his only family see her immediately. She was sleeping soundly in her crib in our nursery when he demanded that we go visit his grandma, 45 minutes away. By that point, I still had not slept more than a few hours in short bursts. I had issues with breastfeeding, she had jaundice, and you know what it's like in a hospital—the moment you drift off into sweet, rejuvenating sleep, they come in to check your vitals.

I was so exhausted that I was nearly delusional when I fell into one of her four hunter green wingback chairs. He left to buy her groceries, since she was wheel-chair bound and we were her only remaining family, and it took everything I had to keep my eyes open. I know her old age was a factor in his desire to go see her as soon as possible, and I understand, but I was livid. I was just absolutely spent. I had no idea how to communicate in a healthy way that I NEEDED to get some kind of sleep soon, and I couldn't let him just take my precious new baby alone.

Sometimes I think this really set the tone for our parenting journey. From day one, when I had to wake him up to hold my legs when they asked me to push, to day five when I couldn't even find the words to ask for the rest I needed, resentment started to chip away my desire to love him.

When the hormone drop hit after a few days home (which I was not prepared for) and I was sobbing in the shower, I was met with an equally uninformed husband who really had no idea how to be supportive, and I had no idea what to ask for or how to even ask for it. I was used to being the rock in the house—no, the entire foundation. That foundation was about to fall apart by the crushing weight of the whole household on my shoulders and me having no idea how to ask for what I needed.

At the same time I was crumbling, my husband was forced to adjust to not only the loss of my time, but the loss of me. The woman who would never let him leave without a goodbye kiss was about to be thrown out with the baby's bathwater. The easiest thing for me to drop was our relationship, at a time when I needed it most.

The Anxiety of Perfection

I love my children. I've wanted kids as far back as I can remember. Of course, all for my own selfish reasons, like wanting to have a loving family and raise kids that knew with every fiber of their being how much they were loved and how important they were. The idea of "sacrificing" for one's child made no sense to me. I knew that it was my own selfish want to bring a child into the world, not an act of selflessness. My child would never "owe" me anything. I owe them everything!

I feel like I grasped from very early on how hard raising children is. I understood the time and financial commitment and even had some concept of how heavy the mental and physical load is.

What I was not prepared for was the emotional and spiritual load—how they would awaken so much in me and force me to fix any area of my life where I hadn't fully stepped into the adult self. After my daughter was a few months old, I realized how unhealthy my attachments had been up until that point, as I mourned who she was every day when I'd wake up to an entirely new version of her. And soon I would realize the massive amount of anxiety I was carrying from each moment to the next, beginning with the day I first got a positive result on the pregnancy test and threw all of my confidence and self-trust out the window.

I was really fortunate to have discovered Conscious Parenting when she was still an infant, as it caused me to start working on my stuff right away. I am so grateful that all she will ever remember is (hopefully) a fairly present, loving mom.

However, before that time, I was definitely an anxious parent. It started before she even arrived. Once she was finally in my arms, the anxiety was a loud, interfering energy always blocking me from my intuition. After we got out of the hospital, breastfeeding was the biggest struggle. I had a breastfeeding pillow that just didn't work for my tall frame at first, so my back and shoulder hurt continuously. Then I had a low milk supply and getting it up became my life's mission. I tried everything, read everything, and beat myself up. My husband gave me grief because she was always nursing anytime we were home. She was our first, and he wanted to hold her too. To him, it felt like I took her back two minutes after he finally got her. It was an exhausting time as I tracked how much I was pumping, tried everything imaginable to increase my supply—from Gatorade and beer to fenugreek pills and medicine I ordered over the internet from some faraway island pharmacy. I was lucky to pump 10mL in 30 minutes every two hours and had terrible headaches from everything I was trying. Yet it never seemed to be enough, and the guilt of having to supplement with formula was outrageous. Even when I was ready to quit pumping at 12 months, I had second thoughts and tried to start up again, so heavy was I with attachment and sadness.

Leaving her at daycare was heart-wrenching, and I'm sure now that I made it worse for her by spending lunches together while she nursed and played, but then leaving her again as I had to go back to work. I know this because it is a scenario she still, at almost five, works out regularly in her play. She is always "leaving" her baby dolls and returning, only to leave again. I'm so sorry Love!

Every ounce of my mental and physical energy went toward her. She wanted to be held non-stop and doing anything at home became impossible. I could barely get to the bathroom, much less make dinner or clean the house. I remember thinking, *Why did no one tell me how much work it is just to carry this heavy child around with one arm all the time?* In all of my preparation and planning, I didn't practice accomplishing anything one-handed. For the Type A, multi-tasking, overachiever that I was, this was like coming to a screeching stop on the highway and being stuck in crawling traffic for the foreseeable future.

Of course, I had a fancy baby carrier, which I couldn't easily put on by myself—I didn't discover my fantastic ring sling until she was older. I thought I'd bought everything I would need, but how does a new mom REALLY know what she needs? Each child is different and even what I recommend today may have been improved upon since I had my children. Yet I think the ring sling is terrific and timeless, and I only wish I had it from the beginning, so losing one arm wouldn't have been such a shock.

Where I'd previously just done it ALL in our home, I was now rendered nearly useless to anyone but her. I couldn't take out the trash, do the dishes, buy the groceries—absolutely nothing was an easy task. By the time I got her to sleep, she'd be up again. It felt like I had less than zero time for myself. She was up as soon as I even thought about waking up, even before my alarm no matter when I set it, and either wanted to be held or screamed the entire time while I got ready for work.

If I wasn't just holding her and trying to do things one handed, or dying inside as she screamed while I got whatever done that needed to be done, then she was breastfeeding, and I was confined to the chair. Worse, I was at work while she was at a daycare that it took me a year to realize was not good for her. It took that many months to be able to trust my perception of what was happening, to weed through the anxiety and clearly see that no, this is not right. I'm not a paranoid new mom. It's not right that they are constantly losing staff and that she seems terrified of the teacher after this many months. This isn't cool, and something better exists.

To my husband, our new life must have seemed like a tornado picked him up and put him in a different house. Practically overnight almost every responsibility either went to him or went undone. The problem immediately became evident as I languished in the chair, desperate for him to even get groceries or to please just bring me a glass of water as I died of thirst. It was the happiest time of my life, ruined by growing resentment, tension, and anger. If he wanted me back, I felt like he should give me some time back to give to him.

Every bit of night duty, every diaper, every task with her was on me. Of course, I made it this way. She needed me! She really did utterly lose her shit though if it wasn't me holding, bathing, or feeding her. She wanted me always, and even now this hasn't changed. With his seeming inability to "properly" care for her, I felt validated in this opinion that only I could possibly be the one to help her. I was way too afraid to actually leave her with him to see if he could learn how to manage, just like I was learning.

Immediately my generous enabling of my husband during our first five years pre-child became crystal clear. He refused or was unable to pick up the slack in nearly every area of our lives. It wasn't that he was cruel, he seemed utterly convinced that he was 100% incapable of performing any of the chores that I had been performing up until that point. Asking him to do any of the additional tasks a baby afforded was like pulling teeth. Yet most of this disconnect was due to our failure to adequately prepare for the teamwork of parenthood and a total inability to effectively communicate needs. Let me be clear: becoming a parent was not the problem, for me. Being so consumed by the tasks of parenting that I was unable to carry the entire load of the house like I'd been doing up until that point was the problem.

So there we were. Exhausted. Confused. Anxious. Guilty. Resentful. Our worlds turned entirely upside down. All of our family were either elderly or far away. No help. Not even a nearby babysitter, and definitely not anyone I trusted with her. Our time together as a couple vanished. Gone were the nights I'd sit in the basement theater with him and play *Call of Duty*. Gone were the late dinners at the fancy restaurants. Gone were the casual runs to Target after 7PM. Gone were the long showers or last-minute trips. Gone was the affection, the pat of his hand on my leg as we motored through the sunshine, caressed by the open air on his motorcycle.

I remember thinking: *Oh my God, that diaper commercial was right! A baby really DOES change everything!*

The fact is, the baby didn't change everything so much as highlight everything that was broken. I remembered all of the times in my dating life that I had secretly hoped a boyfriend would slip up and get me pregnant, and now I could clearly see how that wouldn't have made a single thing better. First, I can practically attest to the fact that being a single mom is exhausting. Second, (and not that this was behind my intention) babies weren't some magic relationship potion that created two loving, equal partners. Men didn't just step up to the plate because a baby entered their world. In fact, I imagine it's closer to the opposite in most cases. And they especially wouldn't make me whole just by their presence alone. I had no awareness all of those years ago that this was an inside job, that I should have done BEFORE even thinking about having a child.

Babies are the relationship x-ray machine. They come along and immediately you can see through the façade to all of the bullshit you've both been pretending doesn't exist. You see anything you tolerated but is no longer acceptable. You see anything you took for granted that you no longer have. And you especially see the worst of each other as self-care takes a back burner it NEVER should take. In fact, you see the worst in him BECAUSE you aren't insisting on having time to take care of you. Without time for you, time for the relationship is the last thing on your mind.

Self-care is the fuel for our tank. When your husband or child takes all of your energy, and you fail to do any self-care, all you're running on is an empty tank the next day. And if those days add up, that means you're going to be in a constant state of stress, and eventually fall prey to anxiety, depression, or physical illness. Just like a car with an empty tank can't be driven, or a fuel-less lawn mower can't mow, you are no service to anyone else if you're trying to run on fumes.

The non-stop presence that a baby requires was positively foreign to someone like me. I was always in the future in my head, always planning and preparing and doing and achieving. This concept of just BEing was alien. I have to just sit here and be available, without a thought in my head? What?! I have to let go of my stories and stop judging everything?! How do I change these thoughts? I have to be patient? What IS patience?

Yet, I learned. I did the work and read countless books, learned how to meditate, learned how to be the watcher of my thoughts instead of thinking they WERE me. I learned how to detach from my identities—as a mom, a wife, an engineer, etc. I learned how to let fearful thoughts go. Eventually, I learned how powerful just my energy and emotional state are. But most importantly, I learned how to release control and drop all expectations.

Conditioned Expectations

At a practical level, say the typical expectation is that the man is the provider, the mower of the grass, the maintainer of the vehicles, and the love machine in the bedroom.

When your husband is none of these things, then what? Well, you start to judge him. You begin to compare him to Becky's husband, or the guy playing the husband on T.V., or every other husband you've ever seen, including your own dad. Then you realize that he's not living up to those expectations, and you start to wonder how to fix it. You begin to remember old partners and imagine them doing those things right now.

Or you become parents, and he's not parenting like you parent. He's not like Becky's kid's dad. He's not even like your dad. He barely lifts a finger. You start to question if you just have unreasonable expectations, or maybe if there's just something wrong with you that is causing this. Are you too soft? Too hard? Too needy? Why aren't you successful at getting him to change? To help?

God forbid you go online and ask anyone (meaning strangers, of course, we don't talk about our shitty marriages publicly with people that know and love us) if your husband is normal or for any advice—they will be telling you to get your ducks in a row before you even have a chance to refresh the page. People on the internet will plan your divorce for you if you let them. You have to remember that nearly everyone on there (and in real life honestly) is only coming to you with one qualification: their experience. This means their pain, as well. It doesn't mean that they've ever spent time examining their own co-creation or role in what transpired in their personal relationships.

Just today I saw a woman in a Facebook group on marriage post about her husband that plays video games all night and is a zombie the next day. She does everything around the house, works full time, and takes care of the kids. *Hi déjà vu, long time no see!* This poor lady was describing EXACTLY my marriage two years ago, and she received 98% "LEAVE HIM!!" comments on her query. If we add all of that noise to her confusion, I'm willing to bet she's looking at her husband with new fear tonight.

So aren't all of those people right? Shouldn't she leave him? Shouldn't I have just left mine? Shouldn't we be allowed to have expectations for our husbands?

The short answer is, no: no one is guaranteed to live up to your expectations unless you are paying them to perform a specific job or task for you. You didn't HIRE your husband, you married him out of love. He's not required to mow the lawn any more than you're required to do the dishes.

The very first task of repairing any relationship is to let go of the roles you've created for him in your mind and accept the man in front of you exactly the way he is. This step is true not only for husbands but for your children and parents as well.

Before we married, my husband used to constantly laugh when I would vent to anyone and say it was all about expectations—meaning that he was keeping mine low. Why I decided after we were married that he should suddenly live up to the ones I'd created in my mind, I don't know. He'd spent plenty of time before we actually slid on the rings letting me know where he stood on the issue.

Resentment

So, when the babies arrived, and he was online all night playing *Destiny* and tired the next day, I would fluctuate between cool with it because it was, after all, what he'd always done, and totally livid because life had changed for me and he should feel the pressure too. I could hear the judgments of everyone around me... The moms online. The friends in person. The co-workers at the office. If I shared the things my husband didn't do, the reaction was surprise, judgment, directions to make sure he did those things or find someone else. LEAVE HIM.

That was when those seeds of resentment sprouted. The seedlings grew into fear, and that fear eventually became a daunting forest of the subconscious intention that the marriage end. I was so angry all the time because the father of our children wasn't bearing any of the burden, that I lashed out and shamed him constantly. I tried to make demands, wake him up, text him to come to bed, make passive aggressive jabs, yell and scream, or not talk to him at all. I felt like I couldn't breathe. I felt like I had no oxygen and I was trapped in a nightmare. I really hated him for all of it, but still not through the conscious eyes of what he should be doing or not doing for me, but what he was choosing to do or not do for his child. In my mind, it was almost like he was committing violence against her by not getting enough sleep to be present with her the next day. I was always hurting and in fear and only saw him through that lens. Everything he did matched this new filter, everything he did was evidence that I should leave.

Once we get to this place, we begin to look at men or women that seem like THEY wouldn't do the annoying shit our spouse does and imagine them in our lives. Or, we just look at the voids and go into depression. Once we check out in this way, the relationship is often doomed. We feel powerless to change any of it, because we firmly feel like the victim and that they are to blame for all of it. This is when we often set the subconscious intention that the relationship fails, which then shapes our reality.

As resentment builds, trying to control it creates defiance. As Carl Jung says, anything we resist persists, so as we continue to see evidence of our spouse seemingly intentionally not meeting our needs, the negative behavior appears to begin to increase. In truth, our filter has merely changed to match our new intention. When both sides are in this place, the lines of communication break down completely.

My husband and I barely talked. We barely acknowledged the other existed, except to bitch about what they were or weren't doing. We lived together in the same house purely for the kids. Even when his job was outsourced and he was home all day long for months, he stayed in the basement playing video games, and I was upstairs, deep in my work and businesses and my spiritual journey. I didn't want to spend time alone with him because it was another pull on energy I didn't have, and he seemed fine with that too. Our one and only date night was a fight about his endless hours of playing video games.

Where, in the days before we made our big move to Ohio and started our family, we used to meet for lunch every single day, and it was a friendly encounter and exchange of communication, we never invited each other to lunch even though we were in the same house. If we picked up something to eat together, we still ate it looking into the loving screens of our phones... not each other.

Once we were to that phase, all of the other things that had previously been tolerable in my book became screaming alarms that this was never going to work. It felt like I was the only adult in the house and two demanding children was all I could handle. Even as things started to shift as I worked on myself and my reactions, I still had thoughts of taking the kids and moving somewhere warmer without him, convinced he would never change, would never make me a priority. In actuality, I needed to make myself a priority.

The resentment toward him was not unlike the subconscious resentment I'd buried toward my own family. In my mind, doing a task that he *should* be doing was letting him win. Just like in my mind, going on a diet was letting my mom win. It sounds ludicrous, I know, but those rebel tendencies we had as children or teens usually stick with us as adults. It has taken me a long time to come to the realization that the only person I'm hurting in that situation is me. It is not about my husband or even my mother "winning," it is about my willingness to love myself. This is a concept that is much easier to intellectually get than it is to embody because for so many of us, loving ourselves is a monumental task. Even understanding what love really is, and opening up to it is a journey that can take years.

Yet, loving ourselves is THE task. If I could get you to love yourself in one sentence, that would be the only sentence you'd ever need to read. It would change everything about your life. The problem is that we have too much junk between us and loving ourselves. There is too much pain, too much hurt, too much shame, too much guilt, too much anger, and too much resentment to even come close to touching that place.

Oh, if only I could go back in time to all of those moments I made a choice that didn't reflect my own worth out of a desire to not be controlled by another. If only I could have seen that my defiance was detrimental. My perceived rebellion was only *me* saying NO to my own life. More on this later.

> *"Failure is an opportunity.*
>
> *If you blame someone else,*
>
> *there is no end to the blame.*
>
> *Therefore the Master*
>
> *fulfills her own obligations*
>
> *and corrects her own mistakes.*
>
> *She does what she needs to do*
>
> *and demands nothing of others."*
>
> — *Lao Tzu, Tao Te Ching*

Releasing Expectations

It wasn't until I stopped caring what anyone else thought and released him of every expectation I had for every role he was "playing" that I could slowly begin to see who he is and accept him for it. I had to turn off the judgments; my own and the reverberation of those around me.

If I shared something about him and heard fear in the person's response, I dismissed it. If I heard judgment, I dismissed it. I became hyper-aware of all comparisons of what is good and bad.

I learned that what he couldn't do, and what I couldn't do, had to be outsourced, or the conditions that created the need for it had to change. If he couldn't or wouldn't help me clean, and I didn't have the bandwidth to do it all, then we needed to hire someone to clean. If I couldn't rely on him to take both kids out on his own alone when they were little, then we needed to hire someone to help him. It took accepting him for who he is to stop my self-imposed suffering and see the multitude of other solutions that were staring me in the face.

Couldn't he learn? Couldn't he do those things? For some of it— certainly. I could probably change the oil in my car, too, but I'm not going to do it. I eventually realized that I can't control him and I can't force or scare him into learning or wanting to step up. I can let it go undone, or I can find someone else to do it. If communication didn't change it, then it's up to ME to decide what I am willing to live with. What is it truly costing me and what are other ways to make it work? How can I inspire him to help, since I have no control over him? How can I more effectively communicate what I'm feeling and what I really need him to do as a partner in this household? Once I presented the problem and asked him for solutions, it was up to him to decide to step up if he could or know that help was going to be hired if he had nothing to offer. Once he realized that I was going to make sure my needs were met, with or without him, I imagine he probably started to do the math and realize that eventually he may be outsourced altogether.

For other tasks, I had to accept that he was doing the best he could. After my second child arrived, he truly was overwhelmed easily by their constant baby and toddler demands if he was on his own. Assuming that he should have the same abilities and capacity for chaos as I do was only hurting me in the end. The fact is that women are naturally wired to be caretakers and men are not. We are attuned to the children that grew inside of us like no one else ever will be. We have an invisible connection to them at all times, and I believe it's far easier for us to quickly understand their needs than it is for the average dad. There are amazing, 100% attuned fathers out there... but I did not marry one, and I don't know many.

The male brain is built differently than the female brain. I've been told that giving men a list of domestic tasks to do actually depletes testosterone, and that they do better receiving one job at a time. They also need 20-30 minutes after returning from work to be ready to socialize, and they can't juggle multiple tasks at once. Further, men release oxytocin, the bonding chemical, through playing with their kids, instead of just looking at them or hearing their cries. All of these facts are things my husband repeated to me or showed me over and over, but I didn't listen. If only he had pointed it out in a book! I can be terribly stubborn... just like him. I feel so silly now for not just researching the differences in the male brain. I thought he *could* be just like me—an impossible task for his sex. Author David Deida postulates that the direct approach I was using in my communication was actually counterproductive because we were both in masculine energy, rather than inviting him into the solution with feminine energy.

Throughout history, the women and elders have cared for the children together, while the men spent their time hunting for food and protecting them. Is the ideal we have created now the best way to live? For us? For our children? Or are we fighting an uphill battle? Were men and women ever really meant to live with each other, especially for their entire lifetime? I don't believe so... especially not without the help of a village behind them. We've pushed away the village, the support of community, and the natural bonds we have with our own gender under the delusion that we can do it all, have it all, all on our own. We have put the village in nursing homes and in houses right next to us that we never enter. Consumerism over connection has set us up for failure in so many ways.

We're working full-time jobs to pay for our big houses and all the shiny new things they can hold, making the commands on our time exceed it. As our children have endless needs, we drop what we can afford to, and push the relationship aside. This is then detrimental if we've used the relationship up until that point to replace our **own** self-care and self-love.

Now, at two and four years old, the chaos, crying, and demands have decreased, and my husband's playful nature—when he's present and tuned in to them—lights up their faces with joy. Being overwhelmed by young children was not him being a dick, that was him just being who he is, soothing the wound of my absence, and acknowledging his own present personal capabilities. With a diagnosis of ADHD with hyperfocus, he assured me ad nauseam that he had a problem and was doing the best he could, it just took me a long time to silence the noise in my mind and believe it. It was up to me to decide if it was something I was willing to accept or not. Now I feel that a lot of the "symptoms" he describes actually sound more like normal male behavior, such as having a hard time shifting from one task to the next.

I can only control my behavior and my reaction to another. If his behavior with the kids was unacceptable, it was up to me to both teach him a new way, model a new way, and not allow that behavior to continue by responding to it in a way that disrupted our old default patterns and forms of interacting.

Dropping expectations and realizing that **the only person I have control over is me** started to change our marriage, but something else was still broken. Something else still needed work, and it took taking him out from under the microscope to realize that the problem was me.

Reacting

In the beginning, I learned how to stop reacting when he did something that bothered me (like existing..some days). From my teacher, Dr. Shefali Tsabary, I learned how to do vipassana meditation and stay on the breath. I learned how to stop being passive aggressive and either too silent or too aggressive, to stop yelling and shaming. I realized that I had to be more attractive than the video games and that wasn't going to happen if every interaction between us seethed with resentment.

Yet inside I still reacted, especially before I started meditating daily. My body still tensed up and burned with anger. I spent many journal pages venting instead of unleashing all of that rage on him. Though I tried to manage my thoughts and go back to the breath, it was like I was noting everything that was happening on his Cons List—you know the mental lists we keep: *"Didn't respond to child in three seconds and made her cry, 4th time this evening."*—then replaying it on a loop in my head.

When his behavior with the kids was unconscious, I would let the kids know and try to move them away from it. That "united front" thing you hear is a LIE. If your partner does or says something unconscious, pretending to be unconscious too does not in any way benefit your child.

Yet I kept using The List as fuel for my discontent. I'd read Eckhart Tolle and knew I had three choices: to change it, to accept it, or to leave, but for a long time, I was clueless about HOW to change it. I thought that meant changing HIM. And the only way I knew how to change someone was to keep attacking, keep demonstrating my disgust and disapproval, because that's what I was shown. Leaving meant major disruption and fears about security, so it always seemed like the next option but not an option at the same time.

I learned more about how we get into these situations and chaotic relationships, and realized I had a lot of evolving to do, and he was the catalyst. As I finished up my coaching certification and first year of training with Dr. Shefali, I began to welcome the growth, the muck, the dismay. Each day was an opportunity to test my expanding consciousness. The more he pushed, the more I was able to go back to my books, go deeper in my meditation, coach myself, and reflect more and more about what this was here to teach me. I had to trace each reaction back to its root, like finding the knot in a tangled mess of yarn. I had to start at the end and keep unwinding, uncovering, unlayering the pain to find the source so I could feel it and heal it. I began to question everything, to welcome every single conflict almost with delight that I was given another opportunity to mature and allow my inner child to heal and recede and my adult self to step boldly forward.

The Loving Choice

The problem with expectations is that our anger over them not being met is a mirror of the anger with OURSELVES for failing to meet our own needs, for failing to LOVE ourselves. I entered the relationship only knowing how to let him love and care for me, I had no awareness at all yet that I was depending on him for something I should also be doing for myself.

I was caught in the delusion that something, I saw it as my spouse, was coming between me and what I needed. I was mad that he didn't *love* me enough to do the thing, or you might say didn't *respect* me enough to do it. Doing it for him would mean that he was rewarded for his shitty behavior, for not loving me. Yet if I looked in the mirror, I'd see that I didn't even love MYSELF enough to do much of anything for me!

They are merely matching our own behavior—matching our own vibration. We haven't shown them how to love us because we haven't loved ourselves. And they likely aren't loving themselves either.

Just this morning, a Saturday, I managed to escape for a long bath. My husband had stayed up until 5:30AM playing some new release of his favorite game... I know because that's when my alarm went off and I heard him coming to bed. By 10AM, I woke him up to let him know I was taking a bath and the kids needed to be watched. It took a while to get to this point, but we have, and he got up a few minutes later and went downstairs with them. When I first started on this journey, I didn't ask for this kind of help in a respectful way. More on this in Chapter 10.

Anyway, I was meditating in the tub but distracted by the piles of laundry and the general wreck of our bedroom. As I have been trying hard to do lately, I asked myself, *"What would this look like if I loved myself? What would I do with it? What would the loving choice be?"* I realized that, of course, the room would be spotless. My clothes, and all of the kids' clothes mixed in with them, would all be folded nicely and put away. So, after I ended my bath, I got to work. It had an entirely different feeling tone from the *should* and *shame* feelings I've always associated with cleaning. Instead, I was doing it because I love myself. And because I love myself, I love my things and the space we're all in together. I feel the energy of my belongings and, in that neglected and haphazard state, they are disruptive. I desire my bedroom to feel loving and soothing.

Though I have been trying to teach my children to pay attention to how they want their space to *feel* rather than insisting that they clean and pick up, I have failed to really understand this for myself, to really shed the voices from my childhood and allow a new relationship with myself and my belongings to emerge. What I've come to know now is that if I desire to put a high vibration item in the room, like a vase of fresh roses, and I feel resistance, then the room's current state doesn't match my inner state.

Anyway, my kids found me shortly after I started. Fortunately, by now they are old enough now to go entertain themselves, so they would come and go as I picked up and sorted. Then my husband wandered upstairs to see what I was doing. By that point the floor was clear, so I started to vacuum with a stick vac we keep upstairs that isn't really for serious cleaning. He suggested we use the normal Dyson and I just said that was a good idea. Before I knew it, he went downstairs and got it, and a half hour later the entire upstairs floor was clean! He even mentioned to me more than once that I "motivated" him to clean and he liked this. For ten years I've tried to convince him to clean the same way my mother tried to convince me, first through direct requests, then fear and shame, screaming and yelling, and even punishment… and of course, it didn't work. The day I really, really, let that all go and just started loving myself, he joined me in cleaning.

It's not easy to ask yourself what loving yourself would look like, but once you are able to see the choice that feels like true love, your life has a different glow. Then the people close to you begin to mirror your love for self. Then you start to manifest. Loving yourself is the only path to any destination matching your worth.

Being an authentic wife doesn't mean the marriage is perfect or my husband is suddenly perfect. It means I've accepted responsibility for the quality of my own life and have given him back responsibility for his. It means that I'm more concerned about doing what's true for me than I am with doing anything that makes him happy, because that is a job that only he can do. Sometimes being true will make him happy. But sometimes it won't, and that's part of a relationship. If it doesn't, it's up to him to discover why. Because authenticity and alignment to my soul means my actions are always right actions, they don't intentionally harm or hurt. They are as real as real gets. The person I hurt when I'm not aligned is me. I stunt my growth *and theirs*. That's actually selfish if you think about it.

Being authentic doesn't mean I feel something for the next guy I meet, and away I go in the name of authenticity. It means I'm always asking myself what is driving my decisions and are they coming from a place of lack or love, of fear or abundance, of hurt or gratitude? Am I paying forward the abundance of love and energy I've cultivated? Or am I a bottomless pit looking for the next person to fill me up, determined to keep searching until I find it?

Until the day I'm able to make myself the priority through a daily, regular practice of self care—self-love—I'm not able to say this relationship is the problem with 100% confidence. Only when I'm so full of love from the quality of my own care will I be able to masterfully discern the quality of this relationship—and devote necessary time to it.

Let the self-care in your life be your guide to how well your relationships will serve you. If you only think about yourself once a month, only eat mindfully once a week, only move your body when you have to and only meditate when it's convenient, then expect your relationships to be equally lethargic, listless, haphazard, and lifeless. They will mirror the quality of your relationship with self. They will be as loving to you as you are to you. There is no abundance coming from another when there's not already abundance within you. If you put yourself on the back burner, so will your husband, and so will your kids. So will your clients. So will your boss. Because if you put something as precious as yourself last, it means those other relationships are either neglected too or totally imbalanced. Only from a place of an authentic life realized will your external reflect the vision you hold for your life. It's imperative to understand this, if only to recognize it as the driving force behind the current state of your relationship. Perhaps then you will not be motivated to leave just to repeat what you see here and now.

Intention + Self Love = The Quality of Your Relationship

Pressure to Grow

Anyone can go through this awakening and do self-improvement and begin to heal those emotional wounds, but there is typically no real urgency to do so until you have a baby (or life-threatening disease or accident). It's as if something clicks inside us the second a child arrives and we are suddenly racing against the clock to get our shit together before we screw them up.

Perhaps it's the awareness that those first six years are the programming years, that everything we show them in that time frame sticks for the rest of their life. The tragic irony is that these are the absolute hardest parenting years and it probably takes at least half of that amount of time for us to heal and rediscover our true selves.

Somewhere inside we know we never want to put the cage around our children's true selves that was put around us when we were their tender age. We want them to never be pulled from the sky and told they can no longer fly, the way we were.

Everything that happened to us in our childhoods is going to surface. Even just watching Mister Rogers again with my daughter brought up a flood of memories and longing that made me sad for days. Things we bury and try to forget are unearthed. When we're tired and our blood is easily boiled, we say things that sound just like our parents or even lash out or punish the same ways we were punished. Then we regret it because we so wanted to be different. We so wanted to be the happy mom that would never dare make her child cry. That puts us in a cycle of shame and blame, and that's a hard emotional state to pull ourselves out of if we don't know what we're doing.

The pressure to get this life thing right, to serve others with a job we love, to be great role models, to heal our addictions—it builds with every day that they grow and reach a new milestone or learn a new word. As they learn to walk, we realize how far separated we are from the joyful presence we had as children. We realize how tragically far we've journeyed from Source, from God, from Love - whatever you call it. Our children are born as close to it as possible, and we realize that we've buried that part of us. We realize that our natural state of bliss and wonder was stolen from our chubby fingers. We realize that our parents, so blind within the muck of their own wounds, passed down the dis-ease of ego, by treating us as less than, as a vessel to regain power, as a portal to feeling loved. We realize that they couldn't even see our real needs through the veil of their pain.

This is a heavy awakening. It is a mourning of all of the years we spent in that fog, of feeling inwardly like an undeveloped child and outwardly like an exhausted, resentful adult. We realize that we never really did grow up. We think about food or chores the way we thought of them as children, eating food in secret or cursing chores. We control our lives down to every last detail to maintain some feeling of power in them. We are mortified by any perceived "mistakes" or "failures," so much so that we play it brutally safe—stoically unwilling to ever be vulnerable. And the greatest catastrophe of all is that we have shut off our hearts, as we were repeatedly exposed to pain so consuming that we block off our very ability to feel. It's time to give love back its original meaning: high vibration energy that is entirely absent of any of the many masks fear wears.

Authentic Action Step #3:

From today forward, release your partner from all expectations, for all roles that he or she may play. Just as you are no longer caged, vow to no longer cage your partner or your children.

Chapter 4: *Love Starts in the Heart*

We don't meet men that we love, for we have no concept of what love is. We haven't felt it in decades, maybe ever. We may have not even felt it in the very womb from which we came. We know our hearts as beating out jets of blood, a way-station in the middle of our chests that we must cleanse from cholesterol and stress or it will cease beating. We have no understanding that love is an energy that radiates from our heart. To know that would be to know pain, and we REFUSE.

We felt pain. It is not for us. We stuff it away with food and alcohol and sex and religion. Whatever we were taught about pain, we repeat, and it is unlikely that we were EVER taught to sit with it until it passes.

Then a child arrives. And that heart starts to do a funny thing. It starts to feel, in fleeting moments. It begins to pulsate with emotion. It starts to reach out to connect with the field around our child. They look at us, gaze into our eyes, and we hear it: "Do you remember mommy? Do you remember Love?" And suddenly, all of the things in our life that aren't Love become glaring reminders of when we built walls around our hearts to survive our parents' projections of their own pain. All of the subsequent pain we have buried and suppressed starts to flood to the surface. We fall into depression, see the lack in our relationships, and begin to claw our way out of the dark.

Once we re-open the channels of energy in our bodies and in our hearts, we pay attention to the sensations our body gives us to show us when we are on the right path.

Once we understand the emotions rather than reject them, what we need to do moment by moment becomes clear. We can pay attention to anger and know we need to hold a boundary. We can feel sadness and know that something in us needs to be healed. Our emotions are how our inner wisdom guides us. Do you have the courage to listen?

True Love

When I was a little girl, I had parents that thought about loving me and did in the version they were taught. They had a mental concept of love. My mom thought about what I needed to learn and experience to be her vision of successful in life. I am grateful and know that they made every effort to raise me to the best of their abilities. In so many ways, I had a wonderful, and undoubtedly privileged, childhood.

I say, "thought about loving me," because I now know that they likely didn't yet have a conscious understanding of what it means to live in and FEEL true love, a feeling that is on the other end of the spectrum from fear and control. Of course, like all of us, they had fleeting glimpses of it. If I was sound asleep, I'm sure they felt love. When I was born, they probably felt love. When all was right in their world, I'm sure love radiated from their heart.

But most of us go through much, if not all, of our lives, thinking love resides in our brain. We think it. We DO it. We read about it. We find evidence of it. We write about it, and we say it and sign it on cards. We don't BECOME it.

Yet, this is exactly what true love is. It's a feeling, energy you generate in your heart that radiates outward. It is actually measurable and creates a field of energy around your body that extends several feet. It is a vibration of a high level, a high-frequency wave of energy. Our bodies are like a cell phone: antennas that send and receive data through the electromagnetic spectrum we exist in. Our body translates those energies into electrical impulses sent and received through our nervous system.

Love is the state that we have to achieve to be powerful creators. It is the state we enter when we are having fun and are joyful, happy, and laughing. I believe it is the state we are in outside of physical incarnation, as the awareness reading this book is just energy that can never be destroyed. Love is the absence of fear. It is the light. It is total awareness and a feeling of connection and oneness to all that is. To me, Love is the same frequency as the Source of all things, which you may call by many names including God or Lord.

Have you ever had a moment where one second you're laughing out of control and suddenly you're just weeping, and you have no idea why? This is super embarrassing at parties! It is because you've activated your ability to feel, and old pain (really any pain that you've resisted) is rising to the surface, wanting out of your body too. You've opened the channel of feelings and emotional energy and they are just all going to come pouring out.

When we go through childhood pain or trauma, meet the unconsciousness of the world, or have our hearts broken, we shut down this channel so we don't have to feel pain. Remember from previous chapters, society is still not comfortable with suffering or the expression of it. We try to avoid it, mask it, and deny it. We refuse to participate in it for fear that we will just be unable to bear it and self-destruct. Our parents likely did everything possible to make us stop making them uncomfortable;

shaming us, yelling at us to stop, hitting us, sending us to our rooms, or distracting us with food, gifts, tickles, or jokes.

If we are in this numbed state, we cannot love, no matter how much we think we do. Love from this place is based on need, dependency, and control.

In this place, we look for others to make us happy, to make us whole. We look to our spouse to meet every need and placate every desire. We stamp them with massive expectations to fill us up. Combined with our ideas about their role as husband or wife, they have entered a job they are monumentally unqualified for.

I think back to my dating years, all eight of them, and blush remembering how needy I was! I was like a puppy dog, so eager to please, but entirely blind to meeting any of my own needs, to loving myself. I wanted a man that was as ready to be as much my everything as I was his. I had no concept of being happy alone. I'd spent 20+ years *tolerating* being alone—very much alone as a homeschooled child. I was so ready to get away from my own family, who often seemed to have nothing but disdain for me, that I was desperate to move in with a man (or have him move in with me) who would love and nurture me in the ways I longed for but hadn't been much of my life. You can imagine how the energy that I brought to those relationships was received—not well. It seemed like anytime I wasn't physically there, bringing my pro-level clinging abilities, they would move on to someone else, or back with an ex who they had previously ranted about. Even with breakup after breakup, I was still blind to it. I instead looked at everything exterior; I must need to be thinner, more interesting, dress better, be shorter, have different hair… I thought how I "loved" *was* what love was! I thought all those men were crazy for ending the relationship, because I was such a catch—they didn't have to do anything! *I treated them more amazingly than anyone else ever had or would*, I was sure. I thought the next woman they chose "loved" them precisely the same way but just looked better while doing it. The shame I already felt for being me was like a gigantic bubble that I wore everywhere.

My weight has fluctuated much of my life, and I was teased at school for that, my curly hair, and being six-foot-tall. Adding those voices to my family's solidified my sense of non-worth and increased my continually shaming inner dialogue. Even though I received a lot of male attention even at a heavier weight, I always assumed it wasn't genuine. Then I received even more when I lost it and thought I was finally worthy, only to realize the same disappointment as relationships blossomed and died seemingly overnight.

It took this contrast, of being so happy in love for a moment and then being utterly heartbroken the next to slowly make better choices. Slowly being the operative word. Okay, maybe not at all?! I went from the guy that would only marry me if I lost weight, to the man that I was madly in love with who met his eventual wife several months *before* we dated—whilst welcoming his first child from another—and must have been with all of us before deciding on her, to a guy that stole my credit card, the one that went back to an ex while I was in the hospital having an emergency appendectomy, then I took a breather for a while, then found another one whom I nursed back to health in the hospital after an accident to find him with another woman bedside the moment I left, and finally wised up and decided I was never dating again. After a nervous breakdown from the last one, due to his gaslighting and denial of his non-stop philandering, I worked on me. I *finally* took that long overdue look in the mirror to realize that the constant here was *me*. Whatever I was doing was not working. So I started to think about what I really wanted, what I really liked. Little did I know, that was only scratching the surface.

One night, I was laying in the bed writing in a journal and suddenly felt the air become frigid next to me. My house was a bit drafty, but this cold air hung like a ball, just right next to me and nowhere else. I could feel its precise edges. I had been writing about men and my heartache and I stopped to say out loud, "Okay God, if you exist, I give. I give up. Please send me a man that will love me the way I deserve to be loved. I won't resist anymore. Please send me The One." I was crying and just let the tears fall until I couldn't cry anymore. I believe it was my dad's mother next to me, but only because she had died fairly recently. Whomever it was, they got the message. I met my husband shortly after.

By the time I met him, I was content, but I wasn't happy. There were several wounds that his presence soothed. There were unhealed pieces of me that delighted in the way he nurtured me. Even the way he enjoyed cuddling made the parts of me that had craved physical touch as a child light up with delight.

He enjoyed being with me just the way I am. I grew up in a home that was very judgmental, that had commentary for the way everyone looked or dressed or spoke or even chewed their food. No one could escape judgment and I grew up feeling its spotlight firmly directed at me. Perfection was demanded, pain was unacceptable, and others were to blame for any unhappiness.

My husband did none of these things. He talked to any and every one. He had no fear of failure. He was impervious to embarrassment. It was like he could look through the shell of others right to their soul, and I felt that immediately. Meeting him was the first time I felt truly seen by another. It was a magical energy, as if we recognized each other at a cellular level. He wasn't critiquing and comparing, he was just happy to be in my presence.

I needed him in order to be whole. I needed him like he was prosthetics for parts of me that were missing. Likewise, he needed me in the same way. Where I was assertive, he could be a doormat (and vice versa, depending on the situation). Where I was detached, he was forgiving. We balanced each other out.

Each human has masculine and feminine energies, sometimes called yang and yin. Masculine (left brain) energies are logical, detached, form-based, doing, decisive, intellectual, and boundary setters. Feminine (right brain) energies are compassionate, connected, being, feeling, nurturing, creative, formless, empathic, and intuitive.

Everyone exists somewhere on the spectrum between the two, fluctuating up or down throughout life. Obviously, men are typically more masculine, and women generally are more feminine, but there is a wide variation that changes based on what our childhoods were like. A child that spends much of its time in survival mode will more strongly develop the masculine.

In my case, we were both very close to balanced, yet my masculine had been more activated as a survival skill (to not feel the pain), and his feminine was more present due to a strong and supportive relationship with his late mother, who was likely quite conscious from what I know of her. She passed a few months before we met, taken by brain cancer six weeks after it was discovered.

Anyway, my intention for marriage was to have all of my needs met. To be comforted. To be soothed. To have those missing pieces replaced. I was lonely alone, avoiding the pain it brought me to be single, unable to feel whole.

I longed for a family where I could feel loved the way I hadn't in my childhood. I wanted to be seen, to be heard, and to feel worthy - the most basic needs for every one of us. I was dismissed as a child the same way my parents were, and theirs, and probably about everyone reading this.

For me, my husband made me happy, and when things started to change and old unhealed wounds resurfaced, that foundation was jeopardized. He no longer was making me happy. In fact, now our dynamic had changed to feel more like my own childhood, and that unearthed hidden fear that had been buried for over two decades.

For him, I was no longer making him happy either. Every second of my attention went toward the kids. Where I needed him to see I was nearly underwater and needed help, all he could see was the huge void left where my presence had been. He also needed to be touched, to be seen, to feel worthy. As the screams of the babies triggered old wounds and conditioning around pain avoidance, we were being tossed like shoes in a dryer, unable to find the way out of this new storm we were in that just kept repeating over and over, day in and day out. No one was there to open the door and stop the cycle.

We were two parts of a whole whose fracture was suddenly revealed, neither of us whole ourselves.

Fight or Flight

Imagine yourself as a young toddler. You have just been caught playing with lotion. You have spread it everywhere and have delighted in the texture of it, the patterns you've made, the pure joy of creating.

Your mom comes in. She gasps! *"What are you doing?! Look at this mess! Clean this up right now! What were you thinking??"*

She has entered fear. She doesn't want to clean up the mess you've made, or even supervise you doing it. She wants this trouble to disappear and anything damaged to be okay. She wants the lotion to return to the bottle and for the floor you have now turned white to return to clean and perfect. She's mad at herself for co-creating this whole situation, by both leaving the lotion in your reach and not supervising you. In her mind, you've just taken something from her, energy that she may not have. Not only may this be clean-up be inconvenient, but she may also view it as time away from her already lacking self-care, or this may be holding up a mirror to her own messes.

You are ashamed, sad, and angry. Your mom doesn't see you. She doesn't see the learning that you were doing or the beautiful creation that you were so proud of a moment ago. She doesn't look past her own fear.

Arguments

When couples argue, the discussions often do not go very far because they are created in fear and project fear at the other. We default to the way we were spoken to as children when we talk to our spouse - yelling, blaming, accusing, threatening, attacking. We gesticulate and shake our hands and slam doors and maybe even throw things or, worse, push or hit.

When we are in this fear state, we are unable to think with the region of our brain that utilizes judgment, our pre-frontal cortex. We are in the emotional part of the brain, or the limbic system, and wound up tightly in our stress response, defensive and on the alert. When either of us yells, we are giving up our power. We have already lost the fight. We aren't approaching the area for improvement as soul to soul seeking to grow, no... we are like rabid dogs fighting. Impulsively circling each other, trying to be big and fierce in the hope that they will cower and run.

From this defensive state, we approach them only from the perspective of, "You did this to me." We don't even see them as another human being, the flesh incarnation of a divine soul, with a myriad of their own experiences, needs, and emotions. We don't even see our own role in co-creating this scenario. Now we're two dogs viciously fighting over a bone.

Lack

That bone is universal - it is at the core of every last fight ever known. It is our own personal lack jar, a.k.a. the ego. If I'm looking at it, it's mine. If my husband is looking at it, it's his. Whoever is looking at the jar sees only their own, and it is EMPTY. Whoever is looking at it believes that only someone or something outside of themselves can fill that jar. The kicker is, the jar is never, ever full. It is a bottomless pit of wanting.

So now we're both standing over this jar, screaming at the other to look at it, to see that it's empty! We are desperately searching for the words to make them fill it, for the actions to get them to acquiesce and do what we want. We try to threaten them into filling our jar. *Can't you see it's empty?!! You haven't filled it! I'm dying here without this jar full! How could you do this to me?!*

Each of us is standing there, seeing the same jar, finding whatever language or action pops into our mind that we think will get the other to just apologize and go fill the jar. While we paint all of the reasons in the air about why they should, they are painting over them with all of the reasons why we should. The air gets heavy and dense with fear. The jars are still empty. No one has seen our need and filled it. Only, while this was happening, our jars each grew. Now, we pick them up, barely able to withstand the burden, and walk through the muddy air blindly. We realize we must fill them another way, so we eat, or we cheat, or we buy more things, or drink, or do drugs. Or we decide not to acknowledge them at all, so we put them down and watch TV, or play video games, or read. We either fill ourselves, consume energy that we hope will fill the jars, or we distract and numb ourselves - pretending they don't exist.

But these jars of endless wants only look outward. They incessantly remind us of all the things that will fill them up; the new house, that expensive designer purse, the latest Italian motorcycle, the new baby with its new baby snuggles. It isn't YOU, they say. It's everyone ELSE. It's THEIR fault you're not happy. It's HIS fault you're not satisfied right now. He SHOULD know how to make you feel loved. You deserve better. This little voice in our head both tries to build us up by putting others down AND reminds us we never have enough. It is constantly wanting more, desiring more, craving more.

We have been raised to believe that the love that seems to fill this jar and make us feel abundant is something we go search for, buy or consume, or altogether avoid. We are convinced that it is a transactional type of thing that can be given to us in exchange for something. When we fight with our spouse, we begin to fear that what we are exchanging is no longer good enough. That must be why it's not working, we may decide. It must be us that's damaged, and now we're not even worthy of receiving love anymore. And with this thought, our jar grows and our heart breaks. We feel it split right in our chest. We are heartbroken.

Our spouse just reinforced a belief we were handed in childhood, that we were not worthy of receiving love, that there is never enough for us. We're instantly back in the body of our toddler self, feeling confused and ashamed on the floor in our aforementioned lotion masterpiece. Our spouse is confirming what our mom or dad showed us, that we weren't worthy of love, and that we should be ashamed for even thinking we were. In a fight with our spouse, we are fighting with the child version of them, at the age they were when they were first told that they weren't enough. Trust that it is not two adults in the room, no matter how it looks or how adult the subject of the fight seems. Your inner child and their inner child are circling the jar, screaming, *"MINE! MINE! MINE! FILL IT! FILL IT!!!!!"* and ready to lash out at anyone that comes near it to take more.

Receiving Love

What are your needs? Yes, love is not transactional. So, what does it mean to receive love? How does one know if they are loved? I read the popular *The Five Love Languages* book almost ten years ago. The book is great, but I believe this concept leads us a bit astray, however. Each of us needs someone to see us, hear us, and treat us as a worthy being. I think the Love Languages book shows us how we *feel* seen, heard, and worthy, but based on the way we were raised and the limiting beliefs we hold. It is not that I need my husband to do "Acts of Service" around the house, it is that I need to be able to have time to meet my own needs, to take care of myself. It is not that I need quality time, it is that I haven't felt seen, heard, or worthy and want his undivided attention so I can feel all of these things. As humans, I think we naturally crave physical touch from the day we are born—it's likely why we come back to these bodies again and again. Touch is a powerful healer and exchange of energy. I believe what our parents did for us as children strongly plays into this concept. I think the idea is that the partner is pointing us back to OURSELVES, and feeling our own love is ultimately what we are seeking.

I have noticed that my very young children do gravitate toward different methods of receiving and feeling love, but it all boils down to: when am I most present with them and truly seeing them for the divine beings they are? When do they feel my eyes? Hear me validate and reflect their experience? Feel the warmth of my love as energy surrounding their body? Set boundaries that align their experience with their worth? Again, when am I most present? When am I attentive and attuned to their needs? I'm modeling how one loves oneself through how I treat them and myself. The beliefs I give them about their own worth and how to love themselves will be reflected in the ways they both hold personal boundaries and feel the love of others as adults. They will feel loved when their partner reflects their own worth back to them, when they point them back to the self-care they really should be able to do on their own. True love does not depend on the other.

Therefore, when conflict occurs in the marriage or the relationship, our mate is seemingly not meeting one or more of those three most basic needs—but we should be meeting those needs on our own. As repeated circumstances enforce the belief that the husband no longer sees, hears, or finds them worthy, the fire is doused. You cannot give love to someone in disconnection. It is not possible. We really need to come up with another word for the love of relationships, because I find confusion there when explaining the state of Love we are in, and loving another, because you can be in that state of Love without giving love to another. We really should just replace it with the word "serve"... but not in the archaic sense of servant, of one being less than. It should be as in each partner, each soul, serving the other to grow. If we are disconnected, no longer seeing/hearing/seeing their worth, we are no longer serving them. So they no longer feel served! The purpose of coming together in connection is for each person to serve the other in positive ways that allow them to grow to their fullest potential. As an intimate partnership, we should be able to both be fully vulnerable with each other and support each other in this raw form, and help carry the burdens of daily life, so each being has the time they need to truly love themselves when the challenges of life inevitably happen.

Self Worth

But before you call the lawyer and write up papers that tell your husband he's no longer serving you, you must understand that no one in a relationship can adequately do these things for you until YOU firmly, unquestionably, wholeheartedly understand your own worth. Others will only treat you to the level of worth you believe yourself to have. If you have a low sense of self-worth, then you will set the conditions for them to treat you as such. They may see and hear you, but not treat you at least equally and preferably as the perfect soul that you are. You have not shown them how to do this. You, after all, feel you are unworthy of almost everything. *You don't take time for the shower you need to take. You don't take time for the painted nails that bring you joy. You don't spend money on the coach, class, or book that you know will help you resolve an issue in your life. You don't spend the money or the time to eat decadent, whole, fresh fruits and vegetables. You don't exercise or dance even though it makes your body feel so good. You don't call in help so you can get the sleep your body needs. You don't keep promises to yourself or honor commitments you make. You don't paint or draw or write even though you're in flow while doing it. You don't play golf or ride your motorcycle or do work in the garage or build a project even though you're in flow while doing those things.* You put yourself last. No, you don't even put yourself anywhere!

Do you see how a person in this place will have a hard time receiving love? They are not even willing to accept it from *themselves.* They already feel that they aren't worthy of being seen or heard. It doesn't matter how many gifts you have to share with the world, until you feel worthy of being seen or heard, you won't be. Not by your husband or wife, and definitely not by the friends, customers, clients, or millions of people you have something to offer to.

Because your parents or school told you or showed you that you aren't worthy, you've wasted away precious days believing them. They were just passing on their misery from experiencing the same. No one but you can decide your own worth - no one! And you are divine! How do I know you are divine? Because we know that everything is energy from the same source, so, therefore, you are the same as what created you—you, the real you, the awareness that chooses where to focus its attention, not just your brain + body. I love Gary Zukav's analogy in his book, *The Seat of The Soul*: he says to imagine God/Creator/Source as the ocean. A cup is dipped in, and that water becomes your soul. Or God is the fire, and you are the torch that was lit in it. You are of God. So know, without any shadow of a doubt, that YOU ARE WORTHY. You are enough, just as you are. And as soon as you treat yourself that way, the world will treat you that way. There is nothing you lack preventing you from being worthy. Anything you believe you lack is a bill of lies sold to you by either your parents or culture. *You aren't skinny enough. You don't have a degree. You're too poor. You don't have any talent. You always make mistakes.* Whatever the dialogue running in your head is, you must kill it, through emotional healing and meditation.

How do you know what is authentic for you? You pay attention to your emotions, the uncomfortable feelings in your body. You are having those emotions, you are not those emotions. You aren't sad, you have sadness within. If you drink coffee, you aren't coffee… you are having coffee. When you are engaged in an activity or conversation or thinking about doing something, and a "negative" emotion comes up, it means something that you are believing right now is out of alignment with your true nature of being timeless energy, of being a divine and perfect being just as you are. When you are being entirely authentic, and not acting from any hidden place of fear, you will not have negative emotions. A negative emotion like sadness, anger, or resentment, means that you are currently thinking a thought or believing a belief that isn't true. It could have come from your parents or culture and is a limiting belief that is out of alignment with your authentic self—out of alignment with your worth.

Abundance / Love

The truth is, the jar is an illusion. It is not real. We are instead in a low-frequency state where we believe that we can not move up without something, or someone to get us there, to make us worthy. We are in an energetic state of lack, a state of fear, rather than a state of abundance, an energetic state of love which is the true nature of life itself. We are out of alignment with the Source of all things, with the language of the Universe. When we're not in alignment, we are blocking flow. We cannot take right action to improve our circumstances because we are in total resistance to what is real and true at this moment. When we are in a place of lack, we are defensive, feel powerless, feel at the mercy of others or our situation. Thus, we continue on in similar circumstances, only clawing out of it slowly and with great effort, rather than allowing ourselves or others to help us rise to new places. We are honestly too afraid of even rising because the pain we know is more comforting than the joy we don't.

Let me illustrate lack versus abundance. Lack: your bank account is low, you just lost your job, and life seems dismal. Fearful thoughts play on repeat in your mind. How are you going to survive? Abundance: you breathe in, realizing you have infinite clean air available to you. You get a drink of clean water, realizing there is no shortage of clean water just for you in this moment. You realize you're sitting in a half-a-million-dollar home, surrounded by things, and can enter your walk-in closet that is full of clothes. You remember your best friend just contacted you about a job that would be perfect for you. You realize that you have more than enough. **Abundance is Love, Lack is Fear.**

Love is not transactional. It is not given in exchange for something else. It is merely an energy we create that starts with our thoughts – a high-frequency energy. It is knowing the jar is overflowing with our inherent worth—nothing can ever make us more valuable than we already are just by being born.

Love is like a **FIRE** inside our chests that warms anyone or anything we are close to, yet we alone seem to douse it when we are frightened or stop tending to it and fueling it. When we are close to others, we receive the same warmth that they generate, the same positive energy, by matching it. If we both have stoked our own fires, then the space between us disappears, and we can become one powerful force in the universe. Others can relight their flame with ours (match our energy), but it doesn't change our fire. Have you ever seen someone light a torch by putting it into the flames? The original fire doesn't diminish, and the torch burns brightly. Love is like that - only WE can put it out, but when we share that state with others it doesn't deplete. We are responsible for continuing to refuel it, to add more logs, and to protect it—which we do by meeting our own needs.

Self Care

That fuel is self care; sleep, making loving choices, doing things we enjoy, creating, music, journaling, learning, reading, dancing, art, beauty, gratitude, travel, exploration, inner child work/healing, meditation, exercise, fruits and vegetables, sunshine, water, nature, etc. Nature is special, because by being with these living objects that already have the fire (high-frequency energetic state), we rekindle our own, or raise our vibration. This is why people keep pets or go on hikes.

Think of your radio – if you turn the dial up you get to the fun music, the stuff you want to dance to. What I'm asking you to do is to turn your dial up to a different station. Get to this higher frequency state, that exists outside of suffering, that exists outside of wanting your present moment to be anything other than what it is right now.

If you have trouble turning up the dial on your own, you can also go take a "nature bath." Sit in an outdoor space, or up against a tree, or float in the water, and breathe in the perfect love of nature and breathe it out around you with every exhale.

We have to intentionally choose to light that fire and keep it lit. This is an energetic space we move to on our own. No one lights it for us, it is a choice we make. No one gives us the fuel. Even if someone tosses a lit match in our direction, we will feel the fire for a moment only until it burns out. We are responsible for bringing that flame back to our own fuel source and maintaining the fire, the light. This is what we experience with food, drugs, sex, etc.: Hot flashes of bliss that do not last. We are desperate for the fire, so we keep taking the lit match, without being willing to move the heavy logs in first.

Or, we neglect our fire entirely, and spend our time searching for logs to give others. We don't even recognize that we have a fire within to tend to. We've been told our fire is not important, that we must just help others build their fire by taking on their pain as our burden, then we can sit in their warmth, that we'll be rewarded for helping them by then being able to shift up from their own overflow. We don't even know we have our own fire. We assume sitting in their warmth IS love. We believe this will fill our jars for a while.

I remember when I realized during one of my husband's "man colds" that he approached being sick entirely differently than I always had. While I suffered along, doing all of the same work I always did attending to everyone's needs, he dropped everything and solely focused on himself. He found medicine right away, went to the doctor sooner, rested in bed and moaned until I would give him snuggles or Sudafed, and generally just took care of himself or asked for help. This concept was so foreign to me, as I was conditioned to ignore my own needs and just keep working, even if that meant I was a miserable person doing awful work and making everyone around me run the other way. I didn't realize that the cold itself was trying to tell me something about how well I was taking care of myself, I just always thought I was unlucky and picked up germs somewhere. The way we as a society are trying to live, overworked and with almost no attention to self care, leaves us with fragile immune systems that don't stand a chance at fighting anything off.

The fact is, we must re-fuel our own tank. Day to day, not only do our bodies use up our fuel/energy, our brains do as well. Imagine that every single thing you do or think causes your inner fuel gauge to move toward E. Work, parenting, cleaning, creating—even exercise—takes some of your energy. If you aren't dedicating time toward replenishing that energy via self care, then your body starts to turn on itself and use muscles or bones for energy. It is no wonder that illnesses are so common when we've been conditioned to believe we can just keep going and giving. We must create time for practices that refill our tank—the first and easiest of those is adequate sleep. Meditation is high on the list too as it not only quietens our mind (which then uses less energy), it helps us regain control over what thoughts or events we have a fight, flight, or freeze reaction toward. Creating time for refueling practices also means that we drop as many needless thoughts/activities that use up our energy as we can.

So when I was sick, a time when my body is trying desperately to get my attention and make me refuel, I was still trying to push through. My husband's "man cold" finally made me realize that feeling guilty for taking time for me was actually selfish, because when there is nothing left of me, everything in my life, including my family, suffers. I cannot give energy that I do not have. Just like I cannot make a donation, no matter how worthy the cause, from an empty bank account.

It's normal to not even know about this fire, this energetic state. While there are other energies around us all of the time, the warmth you generate in your heart that feels like it is radiating outward is Love. It is in alignment with Source energy, whatever that means to you. It is entering the state of unconditional love, raising our own vibrational frequency, the state where we create or manifest from. Without going into an in-depth discussion of Quantum Physics, know that this open-hearted state or frequency of love is something that you can arrive at on your own and it is a powerful state where you can energetically change your reality and the reality of your loved ones. This is the channel you must use to commune with Source energy; as I've said, if you want to call that the Lord, God, Jesus, Buddha, the Universe, or something else—this is the station to tune into first.

Meeting Your Needs

On the other side of raising our vibration, is connecting to our authentic selves and knowing our needs at a deep level. When I discovered the places meditation would take me, I was blown away. I can connect with my intuition, my higher self and more, through meditation. It creates a clear channel, shuts off my brain's ramblings, and instantly elevates my mood. Journaling does this for me as well. This is how I know who the authentic me is, which is vital for setting boundaries, which we'll talk more about later.

I've also looked within to see how I love myself and care for myself after reading *The Motherhood Evolution* by Suzi Lula (another of my mentors), *how* to add logs to *my* fire. I really narrowed down what it is that I enjoy; reading, learning, journaling, art, long baths, swimming, walking in nature, the beach, etc. Knowing how to refill my own cup, replace my own energy depleted by life, is a lesson I wish I'd learned, well, forever ago. If I'd known I could love myself as much as I needed to be loved without depending on anyone else—my parents or boyfriends or friends—to do it for me, it would have saved me so much grief.

So many of us have been taught that it's selfish to think of ourselves first, but that is simply not true. It is selfish to not attend to our own needs first. My daughter came up with the best analogy: You can't mow the grass if the lawnmower is out of gas. She's 100% correct. We have decided somehow we can mow (take care of kids, partners, house, and career) on fumes. In this way, we fail to serve ANYONE. Again: We cannot give what we do not have. We must create the conditions so that we're able to give from an overflow, an abundance of energy.

Now, as a coach and educator, I advise parents to always look to fill up their own tanks first. Just like the flight attendant tells you to put on your oxygen mask before helping your kids with theirs, you must recharge and refuel before expecting to be able to love and hold space for others. But no matter what, we must fill up our own tank first, so our kids and our spouses are not trying to take from an empty tank, and we're not jeopardizing our health by trying to give from one.

Your priorities MUST be:

1. **YOU** - responsibility for self, self care/self love; spiritual, mental, physical, and emotional well-being by replenishing depleted energy
2. **Children** - as they depend on you to meet their needs
3. **Spouse** - they are perfectly capable and should be meeting their own needs, just like you! You can't make time for the relationship until you make time for you.

The rest of your priorities go in concentric circles outward; you'll decide who and what is important to make time for AFTER these top three priorities.

We also need to know that one person can never meet all of our needs. Our husband may fill our need for physical touch, another friend may fill our need to chat over a cup of coffee, we might outsource household chores, another girlfriend might help us with fashion, and a coach might help us really look at our fears and overcome them or help us release emotional baggage we've been carrying around since first grade. The responsibility is on us to ensure that our needs are met no matter what it takes to do that. We must make ourselves a priority.

When we do this, when we become whole on our own, we are attractive. And I don't mean physically attractive, I mean we have a more magnetic pull to others, especially our spouses if we are already married. When I released my husband from the job of meeting all of my needs and started doing it on my own and inviting him to help instead of *needing* him to help, he suddenly surfaced from the basement. He turned off the video games.

I didn't say anything. I didn't make any demands or smash his Xbox the way I had wanted to a few years ago. In fact, stopping the demands is what helped. I didn't threaten or coerce. I just stopped reacting and started loving myself. My being changed. I was lighter, happier, more energetic, more FUN. I was delighted. I was able to see and be grateful for the things he did "right" for our family and find evidence of his love. I could point out the good instead of focusing on what was missing. I was no longer using him for the energy I was unwilling to provide for myself. I was encouraging him to take care of himself the same way I was now taking care of myself.

The weight of my dependence, need, and control had been lifted from him. As I discovered the home inside myself, I realized I would be fine if he were to disappear—sad, of course—but fine. I would be fine no matter what happened between us because I no longer needed him to be whole; whole was somewhere I needed to get to all on my own.

It is true that often we marry our "better half." Then the kids come, and we realize it's a problem that we were a "half" in the first place!

Getting Your Needs Met

Understanding the role you play is vital. Understanding the role their experiences and their own fears and worthiness-killing stories play is also crucial. If your partner cannot meet a reasonable need, then you will have to meet it in another way or with someone else. This could mean they absolutely cannot help you with housework, but they agree that you will jointly pay for a housekeeper or cleaning service. If their jobs or current venture truly are just taking up a large amount of their time and it's essential for them to do this work while the momentum is strong, then you will need to reach out to a friend for dinner or a game of golf where you feel fully seen and heard. If you love to dance, but they are unwilling, you can sign up for a dance class with a friend or meet new people there.

I think it's funny that we as parents can recognize and often remind our demanding children that we can't do ten things at once, but we hold our spouse to that standard of being The One to meet all of our needs, be our everything. That is precisely when we start to feel like their mom. We have set up the relationship to work that way—in the beginning it's easy because we prioritize the relationship and often neglect our responsibilities and other friends to put them in the role of being solely responsible for meeting all of it. When life goes back to the norm, or we are caught up in a treacherous storm of doing after the kids arrive, we slowly start to realize that our needs aren't getting met and we search the room for someone to blame, and that's the closest adult to us.

Shift Up

So now that you have that understanding, we can discuss what to DO when the bone is in front of you, and you are ready to react, attack, or ignore your spouse. The very first most essential thing that you can do is move into a state of love. You may already be in a high-vibrational state and just need to stay in it, or you may have already moved down the ladder to a lower-vibrational state of anger, resentment, or blame, and need to shift up.

Just by this shifting of your body's energy, you are a powerful influencer on your spouse's energy. They will do something called getting into coherence with you—matching your energetic state. In fact, you could end the encounter here and walk away if you feel that it would be best for the situation (such as when they are projecting the day's fears on you). Or, you could stay and wait. Focus on your fire, see its warmth spreading out and wrapping your partner in a loving hug. It is hard to do this without the practice of mindfulness and meditation so that you can control your stress response first. Those are part of the daily habits of self-care and are essential for you to not get sucked into the fight or flight response every time something happens that you usually react to.

Tune In

After meeting your basic physical needs (especially sleep, which we often tend to think of as a negotiable), I highly recommend that the first thing you make time for every single day is meditation. Start with just five minutes of meditation a day and keep working up, either in five-minute blocks throughout the day or one solid 30-minute session every morning or night. While I have been trained to do vipassana (just focusing on breathing), here is a grounding and heart opening meditation inspired by a similar meditation in Dr. Laura Berman's spectacular book, *Quantum Love*. Guided meditations are great, especially if you're new to meditation or it's hard for you:

Turn the Dial Meditation

Relax in a comfortable seated position with your feet on the floor. Close your eyes. Relax your shoulders back, bringing your heart forward. Imagine a brilliant white light (like lightning) twice as big as the space you currently have influence in (like your house, or the conference room, even the globe if you're going live on TV or the internet!) coming in through the top of your head. Imagine that light pushing you down, deep into the earth, with every exhale, into the ground like roots on a tree. Sit in this space imagining this grounding light pushing you down, roots pulling you down as they expand into the soil, until you feel a sense of relaxation in your body. Take long, slow, deep breaths, counting to four with each inhale, hold, and exhale.

Bring a picture to your mind of yourself as a newborn, or think of a time when you felt unconditional love or perfect harmony in nature. It could be the birth of your child, a special date with your husband, a swim in the pool, or a ride on a boat. Imagine it and feel like you are there, really relive it. What do you hear? What do you see? What do you smell? What do you feel? You should begin to feel a sensation in your heart and feel a smile start to form on your face. Breathe into your heart. Inhale the love from the nature all around you and exhale it out into the world. Feel the energy radiate like ripples on a pond out from your chest. Hold this feeling as long as you can.

You may also imagine a fire burning in your heart. This isn't a destructive fire, it's the light of pure love. Imagine yourself putting logs onto the fire. Each log represents your love for yourself, and as you add them, you say "I love myself." You keep stacking more and more as the fire grows, each inhale bringing oxygen to the fire and causing it to become larger and larger. Imagine that you have been under-dressed out in the bitter cold, snow and wind whipping around your face, your fingers aching in pain. This fire in your chest is now spreading to your fingers, to your toes, warmth spreading through every cell in your body. Stop and feel the sensations. Do you feel the warmth? Now it's spreading out into the world around you, not causing damage like a normal fire, just illuminating every space that it touches. Everyone runs to its warmth and smiles, so relieved to feel it again, to see clearly in its light.

Continue breathing, focusing on each breath, trying to hold onto that state of pure love as long as you can, imagining your fire spreading far and wide, bringing joy and happiness to everyone it touches.

Turn the Dial Journaling

Journaling is a fundamental process that we could benefit from regularly doing, but especially when we are in a low state and can't seem to move up. Here are some ideas to help you journal:

1. Vent about your current situation on regular paper. Get it all out. Then move to your beautiful journal and ask yourself "What insight or lesson is here for me?" and write about it. Release (destroy) the vent paper in any way that's meaningful to you.

2. Start each entry with the question "Dear Higher Self," and ask your Self a question. Write the response to it without editing, thinking, or judging it. Just write whatever you hear.

3. Make a point to write down everything you are grateful for every morning. Who or what do you appreciate?

4. Think about the people in your life. Who can you reach out to, to let them know you care? Or, how can you offer them appreciation? Or, how can you serve them?

5. Make three columns on the page. On the left, write "Too Much" and on the right write "Not Enough." Title the middle column, "Loving Myself." Think about all of the things you do or have in excess or to an extreme and fill in the "Too Much" column. Write what the opposite of that would be in the right column. Now, ask yourself what a healthy medium would look like and write it under "Loving Myself." Do the same for the things you don't feel like you do or have enough of, starting with the "Not Enough" column. There's no right or wrong answer; you're looking for YOUR inner wisdom to shine through and point you in the direction of balance. This is a perfect process to help you prioritize decluttering, as well.

Authentic Action Step #4:

Set the intention today that you will catch yourself when you are in a low vibration state, and shift up.

Chapter 5: *Invitation To The Crystal Ball*

I remember so many times throughout my dating life that I just wanted a crystal ball and someone to tell me what to do. I wanted to know what the future would be and what choices I should make.

In life, we think we have no idea what the future holds, or that only a psychic or intuitive can tell us what's going to happen.

This is wrong. You know that saying about history repeating itself? It's true. In relationships and in your own life, you will repeat the same thing over and over and over until you either learn from it and grow or die repeating it. These are called patterns, and that's what a therapist is trained to identify. They go back to our own childhood, so that is why people often expect to be asked about their childhood on the therapist's couch.

We are so comfortable doing the same thing over and over that I've found I'm even prompted by the seasons to repeat the same activities year after year—sometimes down to the exact date.

I keep a journal for both kids that has room for five years of memories on one page. It is no longer even the least bit surprising for me to fill out what we did that day and look back to see that we did the EXACT same thing on that day or close to it the year before—even down to the restaurant we ate at and what I ordered!

I think we kind of get stuck in these cyclic loops because they are comfortable and we're so afraid of change. I love analyzing data (I spent nearly 14 years as a wireless engineer doing just that), and it never occurred to me to take a look at our own data and find the patterns. Now I know that a few times every year on a specific date, my husband enters what I call a mourning period. Now, rather than wonder what the hell is up with him, I can just look at the date and realize it has begun. I believe the weather triggers his subconscious want to repeat activities that bring him fond memories and when he can't because the loved ones he did them with have passed, he begins to mourn. We'd like to think we're in control of our behaviors, but they are really driven by the subconscious programming of all of our early experiences.

Patterns

We must take a look into our childhoods to understand why we are the way we are today. This process is not to judge or blame our parents, or even their parents who passed it down to them, it's to understand why we do the things we do so we can stop repeating what no longer serves us.

> *"Especially after we reach adulthood, we can no longer blame [our parents] for what they didn't give us. We need to take responsibility to raise ourselves to a higher level of maturity."*
> *-Dr. Shefali Tsabary, The Awakened Family*

As the late Maya Angelou said, "Once you know better, you do better." Ignorance and pain are behind human violence and discord. We don't know better and project our pain onward as it has been done to us. We aren't even fully aware of why we may feel the way we do or take the actions we take, as we have been conditioned to believe that behavior is normal or acceptable. Think of all of the laws that people once accepted (like water fountain segregation) that we now look back on with disgust.

We have a responsibility to ourselves and future generations to ask ourselves *why* we do or believe the things we do. Do they come from an origin fraught with fear? Do they reflect the fact that we are all one, all connected, all energy from the same source?

We are working our way through life with what we know, which is what our parents knew, what their parents knew, etc. We also refer to ignorance as unconsciousness, literally being unaware that another way exists. While each generation hopefully evolves and changes a bit, this process of learning through experience and contrast is slow and tedious. It takes knowing that you didn't enjoy something about the way you were raised to try to do it differently, but once you're in the heat of the moment, it's far more likely that you'll default to what you know if you haven't gained the knowledge and tools to do it a different way.

Therapists know that what you saw and experienced as a child will repeat. An excellent therapist, therefore, can hear what you are currently going through in your life and surmise precisely what you experienced as a child. We call this deconstructing. This doesn't even have to be a specific event, just a belief based on whether your basic needs were met: did you feel seen, heard, and worthy?

With a new lover, especially in those early, euphoric, "in love" stages, you often won't see who they REALLY are. But there IS a crystal ball you can look at to see how a MARRIAGE with them would really be...

It's called: Your Parents.

Both of your parents' dynamics will repeat. That doesn't necessarily mean that you will fight all the time then get a divorce and that's it if that's what your parents did. It means that, if you are the wife, whatever role your mom and his mom played, you will eventually play. Whatever role your dad and his dad played, he will eventually play.

In the most general terms, this is typically the role of the narcissist for the man or most masculine partner, and the role of the empath for the woman or most feminine partner. As you read this, keep in mind that this is just two ends or extremes of a spectrum, and we can swing from end to end or be balanced in the middle, depending on the circumstances.

"The Wise Man is square but not sharp, honest but not malign, straight but not severe, bright but not dazzling."

— Lao Tzu, Tao Te Ching

The Narcissist

The narcissists will ruthlessly get their needs met without any hesitation of trampling over others. They will take and take without empathy for the other's feelings or consideration of their needs. They are detached and often use anger to control. If, eventually, their partner stops meeting their needs, they will find someone else to meet them. They may manipulate, gaslight, or charm their way to what they want. They are like a toddler, always in a place of lack, unable to meet their own needs but still desperate for more and for someone to fill them, wanting independence but attachment at the same time.

They always keep people around that make them feel worthy and loved, as they don't have this ability within. They have no place to go inside to meet their own needs. They have blocked their channels of feeling within their body and don't know what it means to enter a state of love, to feel any feelings that they don't feel in control of. Therefore, they don't feel empathy (register another's current feeling state), either at all or very easily. They are looking at the logical side of life.

Oh, they love themselves. But this is coming from the narcissist's ego—the thing which continually judges others to build us up and make us feel better than. That is a protective shell of many layers around our heart that we form mostly in childhood. Their love for themselves is actually entitlement, a belief that others must love them because they are great. This is not a state of true love, of generating the energy of love within, of feeling abundant and grateful, but an inflated sense of self.

The narcissist's scarcity mentality means they don't trust that there will always be enough for them and that others will be there to give it. They view love as conditional or transactional, and they are always chasing it. They feel entitled to having all of their needs met by others. They may burn bridges and can be cruel and unfeeling.

Gaslighting

I want to talk more about gaslighting. This term originated from the 1938 play Gaslight, where a husband systematically psychologically manipulates his wife until she begins to lose trust in her perception of reality. While he searches for jewels from a woman he murdered above their flat, she notices the gaslights dim. When she questions him about the lights, he insists she is imagining it. At the time I'm writing this, we see this behavior right in our White House—with claims like "fake news" or "this is nothing more than a distraction" when we all clearly see the madness. Basically, it's someone trying to convince us our perception of reality is not valid. Losing trust in your own knowledge is very dangerous because then you can be easily persuaded to perform actions that are not authentic for you, that may even be dangerous for you or others.

The most likely reason this could happen to someone is because they already don't trust themselves. The target of the gaslighting probably had a childhood where they were told their perception of reality wasn't real, that they didn't see what they saw, didn't experience what they experienced, or had to keep secrets. Just think of every time you've heard a parent say, "You're ok!" after a fall or insist that a child apologizes to someone who hurt them. They love the parent like a god that can do no wrong and then "love" their partner in the same way, having little faith in their own perception.

In the book *Nasty People: How to Stop Being Hurt by Them Without Stooping to Their Level*, Jay Carter says that only 1% of people consciously use this technique to intentionally hurt the victim; 20% of people use gaslighting as a defense mechanism and only semi-consciously use this technique, while the rest of the abusers unintentionally use this technique once in a while. They may hide things and then make the wife doubt themselves or even feel guilty for questioning them. They can be so convincing that it leaves the brain of an empath swirling.

I know because my husband does this, and I know exactly who he learned it from. He mostly does it over the little things, thinking it's funny or a joke. It can be infuriating and maddening for me. Before I even realized what he was (probably unconsciously) doing, I didn't think much of it besides it being so frustrating. Yet when things were at their worst, I did the math and realized all of the ways he could cause severe damage with this if we were to go through a divorce. I saw him do it with our kids (something as subtle as sneaking a toy from them and saying they must have moved it) and my anger grew even more. While I never entirely fell into the trap, it did poke holes in my sense of trust.

If your spouse does or says anything that makes you mistrust your perception of reality, call it out. Let them know you're aware of it and exit the conversation. There is no point to even trying to get someone to admit that you are "right," it only matters that YOU know what is true. It took me a while to realize that continuing an argument was my own insanity—it was better to stay grounded in reality than to engage.

The Empath

The empath, on the other hand, has zero sense of self beyond being the tireless martyr (often only subconsciously). The fact that they even have needs may never cross their mind, and they would never ask others to meet them. They give and give and give at great cost to themselves. They feel no entitlement and would never think to demand that they are treated with worth and dignity. They have a hard time distinguishing their own emotions from the energy of others, taking on the negativity of those around them and calling it their own. Instead of offering others empathy, they offer them sympathy, taking their pain or troubles on as their burden to bear in exchange for being loved. They don't recognize their intuitive gifts and have difficulty discerning the pain from those around them from their own. They don't realize they can put up a protective shield so that others cannot use their energy to heal. Grounding exercises are important, to keep them in their bodies rather than caught up in the stream of energetic data around them.

Rather than creating conflict, they check out, remain child-like in their need for approval and love, and don't ask for anything—including the ability to do what they need to do to meet their needs. Rather than controlling with anger, they turn themselves into the problem and wallow in guilt or shame. Carrying other's burdens is how they attempt to control. They allow the narcissist to be dependent on them rather than taking any action to change things. They believe that meeting the needs of others is necessary in order to be loved: Give to others, take their pain, and you will be loved in return. They feel RESPONSIBLE for other's emotions, even though that is impossible. They feel shame or guilt if "they make" anyone else the slightest bit unhappy. The empath feels personally responsible for other's happiness to the extent that the empath actually enables them, thinking it is the only way to help them, rather than realizing that other adults are perfectly capable of supporting themselves should they ever be motivated to do so (hint, hint).

They are actually very cruel—cruel to themselves! They think it is too hard to step into who they truly are, to even use their own authentic voice. They shrink, afraid to be big and seen, be vulnerable or make a mistake. They are asleep, not awake to the present moment but living in the past or future. They would rather tolerate the comfort of their familiar discomfort than tolerate the uncomfortable unknown of taking action to change it.

Emotional Enmeshment

Before you can even start to change anything with your partner, you first have to find empathy for them and yourself, and that can only begin by understanding where both of you came from and dropping any ideas culture has given you about the way things "should" be. Empathy is not feeling sorry for them or excusing bad behavior, it's being able to walk in their shoes to understand what they might be feeling and needing. It is not to provide sympathy and carry a burden for them or enable them, but to not react to them with fear.

For a long time, I thought emotional enmeshment, or fusion, was completely normal. I was taught that I was responsible for other's feelings. I was taught: *If I feel sad after you did something, then you made me feel sad. You should feel guilty and shameful for making me feel sad.*

For example, I was shown that if I didn't get the right present or if I said the "wrong" thing, then "I made" my family feel every negative way that they felt. I was taught that I deserved whatever they then used to also make me feel bad—the silent treatment, tears, criticism, etc.

You need to understand that no one is responsible for your feelings but you. While your feelings are valid and should be felt, they belong to you and are based on your own unique experiences and perception. Our thoughts generate our emotions, and no one can dictate your thoughts. Sure, they can try to—they can try to say that you're a horrible person or you always do dumb things—but you can see those thoughts for what they are: the projection of their own pain onto you, and allow them to bounce off and disintegrate.

For example, a child could make you a gift. You can either look at it with disgust, thinking they should have spent more time or money on it, or you can be incredibly grateful that they loved you enough to make you a gift. You are in control of how you FEEL about the present.

Likewise, if someone gives you a gift that is passive aggressive or really more of a burden than a gift, you have the right to release it from your life. There is no responsibility on your part to take ownership of THEIR feelings.

When we're children, especially in the 0-6 age range, all of those thoughts our parents spewed at us became our own programming. So now we do things like think we're responsible for other people's feelings. Our default reactions are based on the programming we received as young children. They are based on our own unhealed wounds and programmed judgments.

It may sound cold or detached, but I promise you that you are not capable of controlling another's person's feelings without their permission—meaning they, alone, are in control of them.

Please release yourself from thinking you are responsible for how they feel, no matter what you did or did not do, or how you did or did not do it. You are giving yourself far too much power. Here's a recent example: I've launched a new business that serves my fellow coaches. One of my friends reached out and admitted that when I announced it, she was quite upset; it was an idea that she had as well. Was I responsible for her being upset? No. I did something innocent. She's quite conscious, and after she sat with it a while, she sent a message to share her original upset and then express her love and support. I, of course, begged her to join the team as I know the power of collaboration. Can you imagine if no one ever made a move that might make someone, somewhere uncomfortable? Nothing would ever get done!

How one feels is based on their own emotional blueprint and perceptions; what experiences they had as a child, what kind of environment they were raised in, and the belief systems they've gathered from parents and culture. If your boss fires you tomorrow, you could be furious and hurt. But what if you had been looking at another job already and just needed the push to leave the comfort of what you had? Then maybe you are relieved. There is no formula that says when X happens, feel Y. The sum of your own experiences dictates your personal thought about the situation and how you will feel. And even then, you have the power to change the thought and accept the situation rather than react to it. *Ok then, I've been fired. Time to look for a new job. I'll enjoy some time off.*

To be able to step back and look at our present moment without assigning it a story, we must be able to shed the ego, or protective shell, that we created in childhood as a survival shield against pain inflicted by our parents or culture. We must be able to view the situation from above.

Knowing how to change my own reactions and projections was the easy task. Learning how to not accept responsibility for another's feelings was and continues to be the supreme challenge. My husband can viciously rattle off four things that are making him upset, and even though I can now see how he created all of them and he's actually just angry with himself, my fight or flight response is automatically triggered as I feel his energy enter my body. It takes everything I have to not be defensive and lay out how his choices created the situation. That's not what he needs from me, and it would only escalate the upset—he's, in fact, looking for someone else to take his pain, and now I refuse to take it away from him.

Eckhart Tolle calls this the "Pain Body," and he says that it feeds on negativity. Imagine it like a dark cloud, surrounding the person complaining. It wants to get bigger, have more power, feed on your energy. If you engage, then it grows into a full hurricane and finds a new home in anyone in the room that is susceptible to it. Weakened energy, or low energetic states, will make you more susceptible. Everything is just energy. If you, instead, let the storm rage, watch the lightning flash and hear the thunder drum, but don't run out to strike your fist at it, then the tempest empties its rain and floats away. You have blue skies again.

Enabling

As empaths, we are fantastic enablers. We can't even see how enabling someone can prevent their growth, because we don't see them as capable. We view everyone, not just our genuinely dependent children, as needing help. We feel INCREDIBLE guilt when we don't drop everything to do what they need. Rather than letting them face the natural consequences of their actions, we step in and save the day, repeatedly. Often, with men, we are afraid of the tantrum if we don't. We would rather just do whatever they're used to us doing than face their rage. They may break things, yell, or slam doors. We'll hear how awful or selfish we are.

"How could you?" "How dare you?" "What were you thinking?" They shame and blame with piercing arrows that squarely meet the bullseye of the scars we've worn since youth.

If you remove their responsibility for loving themselves, they will stay in a state of lack and dependence on you, and you will be overwhelmed by a burden just too big for you to carry. That will then fuel resentment as your own needs go unmet.

Loving someone means creating the space for them to love themselves. Let your husband do his laundry. Let him apply for his own jobs. Let him organize his personal papers. You're doing that, aren't you? Why is it acceptable for you to evolve but not for him to? Let go, and let them grow.

Giving Myself Away

Thank you to my beloved wisdom teacher, Dr. Shefali Tsabary, for helping me to see that I've spent most of my life excessively stuck on the side of empath.

I know that I was taught this most of my early life: *I don't have needs. Give to others, take their troubles from them, this is how you will be loved. You're responsible for how I feel, and you must change to make me happy. It's your fault I'm not.*

I remember getting money from some relative and giving it right to my brother. He was suddenly nice and kind to me, so I learned to give away money to be loved. Giving or doing for others was praised. I was shamed for having needs, shamed for being sad, shamed for being happy if others weren't.

I remember my parents smiling if I did something that made them laugh, or delighting in any of my achievements, when the rest of the time we were often criticized or corrected—an unfortunate side effect of well-intentioned homeschooling efforts. If I was more mature than them—my wisdom too much—they would poke holes in me, eroding my confidence. I learned to shove my authentic self away, because their pain from it meant I would suffer as well. I learned that I had to do something special, something they wanted for themselves, to win their approval. Remember—this is what I learned, not necessarily what they thought they were teaching or modeling. This is how deceptively hard it is to parent; wounds are unconsciously passed down in a moment. There are plenty of parenting books with pages of instructions that will create these hurting, sad parts in our children. Any time a parent refuses the child in front of them, but embraces a false, conditioned version of that child, lifelong wounds are formed.

I also had no idea that I was highly emotionally empathic. I could sense the feelings and moods of others within my own body. I took on their emotional pain as my own or would feel tremendous guilt if I didn't. I was made to feel like I was personally responsible for anything negative anyone else was feeling as a result of my existing. The guilt was paralyzing. The fear of being authentic was oppressive. I was terrified of others, walking on eggshells most of the time to make sure everyone was happy and I would continue to be loved.

In my childhood, I was the annoying one, and my older brother was the physically aggressive one. Almost any attempt at just being me was met with anger and then whatever he had to do physically to get me to be quiet or move out of his space. If our dad was home and saw it, he or both of us were spanked. My father was just doing what he was taught. I only share this because, while I was never in an abusive adult relationship, I have feared men, including my husband, as though they are going to be abusive if I make a wrong move—if I walk boldly in my true path rather than quietly walking in theirs. This is a pattern I've carried with me due to the fear I experienced in early life. To get a man, I carefully tend to their path, then am terrified to veer from it. I have felt like an accessory to their world rather than an equally powerful captain of my own.

All of my early relationships were me fixing, enabling, holding pain. It was like I would stand in front of a man and let him throw every burden on me. I could carry them all. If I take them all, will you love me? Will that make me worthy? What do I have to change about myself to be acceptable to you?

I'm sure that as you're reading this, you also find that either empath or narcissist resonates with you more than the other, but these are two extremes between which we swing. Rather than resting comfortably in the middle, we pull back to the extreme empathic side at times, and others we push forward to the extreme narcissistic side, usually when we're fed up. In the middle, we're balanced. We set boundaries when needed, but we are open to all that we are sensing and feeling, using it as a teacher and guide but not taking it on as our own if it is not.

As I've talked to my mom about her family and my father's, I can clearly see the warning signs. They are right there. Of course, when we are young adults, and especially in love, we don't look at those things. We think we are going to be different than our parents and just choose better. We don't realize the choice has already been made by the fact that we are their children.

The truth is that we carry the survival skills we learned as children into our relationships. We carry generational patterns, the patterns our parents were given and they, in turn, gave us in early childhood, right into our marriage, unconsciously.

My father left my mother when I was eight. To me, he seems very rigid and organized, analytical and predictable. He thrives on routine. He is a doer, always in motion, planning his time and getting things done. My dad was not around, for most of the years that I remember well, and I don't really remember him being around (though physically he was) before the divorce, either.

My mother feels like the opposite in many ways, though she was a perfectionist in her career as lives depended on it. She is more relaxed, not a manager, usually goes with the flow, and enjoys nature. I don't think she's touched a planner in her life. I don't remember much structure or routine. As a homeschooling mother and a full-time emergency room nurse, she took care of everyone before herself.

I have both of them in me, and it has created constant internal conflict. I have the desire to have stronger boundaries (with myself and others) and often fail to implement them. I am a strong emotional empath and spent years blocking it, swinging to the narcissistic side, toughening up to life's pain and driving toward success in my career no matter the cost. I became utterly unwilling to ever be vulnerable or make a mistake. I shut down my heart and forgot how to love.

My husband was actually more empathic than me when we met. He wasn't cold or detached, as his world had been relatively kind to him up until that point. After a sudden series of abuses, death, and tremendous pain, he started checking out and swinging to the other end of the spectrum. He left most of the chores to me, everything but mowing the lawn really. I have often felt, especially before this work and my transformation, like a single parent. I chose a husband that would help me with the dynamic I lived with AFTER the divorce—I picked a husband that would essentially feel absent. My triggers (times when I'd have an overreaction to a stimulus) were related to situations that reminded me of this dynamic.

My mother-in-law did everything for her only son. She didn't let him lift a finger from what I gather, other than to mow the lawn. She cooked and cared for everyone and was very generous with her money and time, casting aside her own needs. When I'm not doing absolutely everything for my husband, he is triggered by not having been given the skills and work ethic to take over these duties by his mother, who enabled him to sit back and enjoy his life as an only child. Up until now, I've also carried her forgotten authenticity; her ability to love and honor her own needs first, her knowledge of her worth and her demand that the people in her life reflect it.

One cause of tension in our marriage has been when I want to do something or take the kids somewhere and am met with resistance. My husband would put up this big fight out of seemingly nowhere, even if he had nothing going on and it was something he would enjoy doing. It didn't even matter if he didn't have to go—he didn't want me to go do anything without him, either. Literally just this week, he shared a detail I haven't known the entire decade we've been together: his father did the exact same thing to his mother. We were sitting at the fair last weekend, and he was sharing how much he loved coming as a child, and then dropped the bomb that his mom used to insist that she was taking him to this exact same fair and was met with her husband's tyrannical opposition—every year! She would yell back that she was taking her son whether he liked it or not and eventually they would all go. I couldn't believe he'd never shared this detail before and couldn't believe we were repeating it, 30-something years later.

I Saw the Sign

So, if you want to know if your husband is going to help out around the house or if you're going to feel like his mom, ask about his childhood. Meet his parents. Unless you've spent years deconstructing your own patterns, look at your family as well. Dig in deep with specific questions and take notes!

Does this mean that if you meet his parents or learn about his childhood and are repulsed by what you see or hear to run for the hills? Maybe. If we were honest, that's exactly what we would do. If close to 50% of marriages end in divorce, save yourself the trouble, and any future kids the heartache, and end it there. Unfortunately, this is not going to be the case until you resolve your own leftover patterns inherited from your family of origin.

However, if you both can meet the parents or discuss the childhood and learn about family dynamics, then you are both armed with some pretty useful knowledge and a glimpse into the future. You can decide that your journey together is going to be about evolving out of these patterns. You can say: *I am not going to change you and you are not going to change me, but I see that, through this relationship, we are going to challenge each other to grow. I'm ready to point out when something is stunting your growth, and I want you to do the same for me.*

For an empath, that means you are going to learn your worth. You are going to learn how to set boundaries—meaning show up authentically, loving yourself, in every moment without carrying other's burdens or allowing treatment that doesn't reflect your worth. You are not going to do for others what they are capable of doing themselves. You are going to learn how to receive love. You are going to learn how to not take on everyone else's energy, pain, and problems, but use the energetic information you pick up to connect with them and offer empathy.

For a narcissist, you are going to learn how to be self-sufficient. You are going to learn how to respect boundaries and have a healthy interdependence with others without depending on them. You are going to learn how to meet your own needs and take care of yourself. You are going to learn how to give true love and feel empathy for those around you.

Essentially, you will both learn how to maintain an even balance of power. No one will be weaker or more powerful than the other. The combined energy of your relationship will be as stable and healthy and whole as each of you.

Stop Doing It All

When I removed him from the picture and started doing things the way I wanted to, when I started being authentic, the stress lifted. Now, this isn't to say that I removed all consideration for his wants and needs. Perhaps it did mean that I withdrew in the areas where he was dependent on me, but that was an essential lesson I had to learn: loving someone does not mean enabling them. In fact, it means the opposite. Just as I was capable of healing and becoming whole from within, so was he.

Nurturing him or our relationship didn't mean being at his beck and call at all times. It meant stepping back and allowing him to step up. It meant knowing that he was perfectly capable in his own life, and this role I'd taken on as his wife-mother, was only hurting both of us. I wasn't a good wife because I mothered him, I was a good wife because he delighted in my company. I didn't need to cook his dinner or wash his clothes to make him feel loved. I needed to love myself, so my energy was enjoyable and fun to be near. He needed to do the same work. He needed to take responsibility for his own energy, have the freedom to fill his own tank with self-care, and be unafraid to be authentically who he is without any constraints or restrictions imposed on that by me.

I stopped reacting to his behavior and started seeing what it triggered within me and how I was responsible for co-creating it, instead.

Let me tell you, it is no easy task to stop reacting when it is all you've known all of your life. It was no easy task for me to turn off the raving lunatic or let him have the last word. It was incredibly hard and only made possible by my commitment to daily meditation and staying "on the breath" when my body entered the stress response. Now I know immediately when I've been slacking on my meditation practice by how much I react to all of the little non-issues of daily life. If you want to change your life, I believe strongly that 20-30 minutes of daily meditation is a requirement. Just vipassana, or giving your brain the job of focusing only on your breathing, is better than taking almost any pill. Not only does it release lots of feel-good chemicals like dopamine, serotonin, oxytocin, and melatonin, it is a necessary mental exercise we need to do to re-program our subconscious and our default responses. Start slow with just five minutes throughout the day, and build your way up to longer sessions.

The Turmoil of Change

As you find the courage to declare your worth and create the boundaries that serve you, you can and will shift the dynamic in your existing relationships. Unless your partner's unconsciousness disgusts you (or affects your health or well-being), I recommend you stay with them as you learn to do this. You are welcome to leave, but know that you are unlikely to fully step into this worth until the next partner, also, helps you see the contrast. It is not something that you can just easily flip a switch on overnight. Situations will come up which present new ways for you to honor your worth as a sovereign being, and each time you find the courage within to change your usual response to one that fully serves your soul, you will regain and rebuild your true power in authenticity.

The only downside to doing this learning with your current partner is that it will take some time for them to adjust to the new you—months or even years. If you're the empath and they're the narcissist, they will fight you with threats, tantrums, yelling, and a healthy dose of projectile vomiting their fears all over you. If you can brace yourself and be unfazed by this, they will slowly adapt to what they'll perceive as the "new" you. As they come to meet you in realizing your worth, they will gradually remove any words or actions from their being that no longer serve you.

If you're the narcissist, it can feel like they no longer love you when they stop doing everything for you. You'll be forced to grow and adapt and realize they've stopped catering to you BECAUSE they love you. It may feel like they're abandoning you, and that can be scary. Learning how to meet your own needs will be a challenge at times, but it's worth it.

Emotions as Guidance

Emotions are energy in motion, ignited by a thought. The energy itself passes through us in around 90 seconds—if we let it. We usually seem to experience it much longer because we continue to relive the thought on a loop rather than sitting back and observing it without judgment. Rather than give ourselves compassion and empathy for the emotion, we get stuck analyzing it.

If you aren't consistently making yourself a priority with self-care and refueling your own tank, those thoughts will come so quickly you won't even realize you've had them. If you're already exhausted from lack of sleep, and your child starts to whine or makes a mess, you may go to anger so quickly that you aren't even truly aware of why... The energy with the thought is anger because you need to set boundaries—in this case, for yourself, to take care of you and refuel so your child's entirely developmentally appropriate needs and reactions don't feel like another burden on you. If your energy tank is full, you won't react to your husband not doing his responsibilities with charged thoughts, you'll be able to respond instead.

However, there is something to be said for strong reactions. What I've seen over and over again, in myself and others, is that the body will shut down if you are refusing to love yourself, understand your worth, and set boundaries. Sometimes, this may mean it walks away, it's silent, it gets so sick that you have to stop, or it refuses touch. Other times it may dramatically voice all of your concerns, finding the tone, language, and action that will speak to the person that has been treading all over your personal boundaries. If you refuse to stand up for yourself for whatever reason, your body will eventually do the job for you.

So when you have a stress response that isn't going away no matter how mindful you are, that is your higher self's way of letting you know that you have got to make a change or demand a change. It is those times that you have got to identify what it is that you genuinely want and need. It is those times that you've got to have the courage to make a stand and be willing to meet your own needs no matter what that takes, even if it means walking away.

Boundaries

Boundaries are your internal compass steering you in the direction of self-worth. They are not expectations for the other! They are you moving away from or toward something based on whether or not it serves you, whether or not it reflects your love for yourself. Your number one priority is to love yourself in mind, body, and spirit. Anything that doesn't reflect that love needs to be moved away from, with a wall—or boundary—placed between you and that behavior. There is no guilt in this process, though the narcissist will undoubtedly try to guilt you for daring to meet your own needs.

Say a boundary is that your husband speaks to you respectfully. This doesn't mean that if they start to yell they might as well have signed the divorce papers, it means you move away from that behavior—as many times as you need to for them to change it or until you're ready to leave it. This means physically walking away, ending the phone call, going for a walk—whatever you need to do to get away from it. They are talking to themselves, vomiting their own pain, and it has nothing to do with you. Find a space that reflects your worth as soon as you are able. "I will not be spoken to that way. When you are ready to respectfully discuss this, let me know."

As mothers, I think we all have a boundary that anyone around us treat our children with love and respect. If someone is disrespecting your child, it means you let them know that their behavior is unacceptable and remove your child. The catch is that you have to do this from a state of love, not from anxiety or fear. From a state of love, you'll know if the behavior is a reflection of your worth or not.

I began this evolution last summer. It was not easy at times, especially with two little kids involved. I'm sure my neighbors can attest to the shouting. One day it would be a desire to go to the mall with my antsy little ones and my husband helping out a woman (by taking her motorcycle on our trailer to an upcoming track day, an agreement I barely knew about) who didn't arrange a way to get home. After waiting all morning, instead of putting off my plans further for this bizarre situation unfolding in my driveway, my kids and I left. Over an hour later he called, bewildered that I'd just abandoned him and dared to eat lunch even though he was so hungry. In the past, I would have waited like a "good wife" for him to be ready to join us. If I did have the courage to leave, I would have still felt guilt and fear during this phone call. Instead, I was short. He was interrupting my time with my children. "This was your choice," I reminded him.

Another time I wanted to take my daughter to a Princess Ball at the invitation of my friend who is his best friend's wife. Even though it had nothing to do with him, he fought the whole idea of it, then said he wanted to stay home with my son, then in a tirade demanded we only go in his van. As we have had many uncomfortable drives where I've felt trapped (during that time in our relationship), I insisted I wanted to take both kids in my car, and he was welcome to join us or not. Eventually, he jumped in and later enjoyed his time with his best friend and our son.

I went from being fought over anything I wanted to do—and I do mean anything—to doing whatever I want. It used to be a battle just to get food to offer any guests we were going to have or to go somewhere I wanted to go. It was a battle if I wanted to turn right instead of left. Deciding where to eat was a monumental task. He would even fight me on how long I could stop to look at something in the store, leaving me without a cart more times than I can count. I parked in the wrong space. Didn't consult him before picking up food. Drove too fast, drove too slow, wanted to take the kids out, wanted to stay home. Almost every little thing was a battle. I was so damn afraid to just do whatever the hell I wanted to do that I let myself become a prisoner in my own marriage.

The more I let him know what was and wasn't acceptable and showed my determination in meeting my needs in whatever way necessary, the more he came around to meet me at my worth. I realized it wasn't loving him to change, morph, or abort my plans all of the time in the name of "compromise." It was almost as though I would squeeze me out of my body and shove in this perfect robot that he wanted, that would make him happy. It wasn't even me that he loved by that point, it was this alter-personality that acquiesced to his every request. As I began aligning to my truth, I imagine he had to mourn the death of the woman he thought I was, had molded me to be. It was up to him to decide if he wanted to live with the authentic me, or not.

"Be BOLD, be who you ARE, then see who loves you."

— Dr. Shefali Tsabary

Trust

As I kept peeling back the layers to find what was at the heart of our issues, I discovered that I no longer trusted my husband. I started to wonder what the mirror was in me, or what I needed to work on, and asked several of my peers and Dr. Shefali about it in one of her classes. I was asked whether or not I trusted myself. At first, I thought that was a silly notion, of course I did. But then I realized that no, I indeed questioned everything. If I wanted to do something, I wondered if I was selfish for wanting to do it. Something as small as getting food to serve guests put me into a tailspin about whether that was normal or not once he pushed back.

Because I knew from examining patterns that I had a lot of belief systems I needed to let go of, I doubted everything. There was no place where my lack of self-trust was more evident than in my parenting. As soon as I knew that the health of another human was in my hands, I started to trust everyone but me! Because I had no experience, I assumed I had nothing internally to go on.

This couldn't have been further from the truth. We each have infinite wisdom available to us at all times. We are physically guided by our feelings. When we're in an energetic state of love, the right thing feels good. Always. Not in a pleasure kind of way, like okay this chocolate cake feels good to devour, but in an, *I have no negative thoughts about this whatsoever and feel like I'm in flow while I do it* way. It takes a while to get to this place where you can hear the answers so loud and clear. It requires meditation to clear the mind of the chatter, and it means sitting in silence and getting back in touch with our bodies fully to feel all of the subtle sensations.

Personally, I'm able to connect with my higher self and Guides for wisdom through journaling/channeling/automatic writing, but you may find answers in a dream or a sign as well. The knowledge we each have available to us is infinite. We only receive it to the degree that we are willing to tear down any walls of doubt or resistance we've placed in front of it. A great exercise is to fully vent about the issue to a coach or in your journal, and then ask yourself what insight could this situation bring you? What is the truth? How is this here to serve you?

Intuition

I share the story often of how I learned at a very young age to pay attention to my intuition, what I call a little voice, that holds a wall up between me and what I'm about to do very briefly and says: "Are you sure you want to do that?" Once, I was traveling with my mother and brother, and we stopped for the night to stay at a Howard Johnson along the way. In the morning, I was awake before everyone, so I decided to take a shower. As I was closing the bathroom door, I started to lock it. This voice popped up and said, "Don't do that." I ignored it and locked it anyway.

I turned on the water, climbed in, and shut the glass doors. Suddenly, the water was scalding hot, and there was no way to escape it—the glass doors wouldn't open at all! I started screaming, terrified.

For some reason, the night before, my brother had been playing with the door and discovered that he could unlock it with a coin. He unlocked it, and my mom burst into the room and rescued me from the water.

Since that day, I've paid attention to that voice, and every time I haven't something has happened. Gary Zukav says in *The Seat of The Soul* that intuition comes from our deceased loved ones, spirit guides, and Masters (angels or higher). I know that when I tap in, they give me brilliant advice and save my ass, so I don't care who it comes from but I know without a doubt that it's critical for me to listen to.

If we shut down this information, including the precise information our bodies are trying to give us (including physical ailments), then we are rejecting our own internal compass. Once we do that, once we sever our actions from the guidance of our higher self, we will learn lessons through contrast. Meaning, we will experience what we *don't* want to learn what we *do* want.

Open up those channels again, and you will learn *before* you experience the consequence. Once you trust your own body and intuition, you will make the best decisions for you that serve you and those you love.

Once you open up to the non-visible information all around you, you'll realize that you have gifts of knowing, feeling, or sensing information about others. You may feel sad just walking past someone else who feels sad. Or you may sense that you know what a pet needs from you. These gifts are present to some degree in each of us, and it's not voodoo or magic.

Just as we are energy, each of our thoughts and emotions is energy, all residing on different frequencies. It makes total sense, therefore, that we have a bevy of information around us all the time. So we don't go absolutely mad, our brains have varying strengths of filters that sift through all of this and just give us the information we want. They parse the data and discard what's unnecessary, for most of us. This is similar to how a cell phone works; though all of the information is around it at once, it tunes in to a specific channel and filters out the rest. The same way every station on the radio is available to you at all times, but you only hear the song playing on the station that you turn the dial to.

Our brains work the same way. Some people, like those with ADHD or on the Autism spectrum, are suspected to have far fewer filters. With all of that extra information, they are quickly overwhelmed and overloaded with data. Others seem to have thicker walls between them and the data coming in, such as those with ADHD with hyperfocus.

Can you imagine picking up on the feelings of people four states away? There's a good chance you did and didn't realize it. A great book for exploring this further is *The Spiritual Power of Empathy* by Cyndi Dale.

So, especially as mothers that already tend to be more tuned in to these energies, we have the ability to know what our child needs from us at any time if only we are present and attuned to them. We can't recognize a sensation, feeling, or knowing if our minds are stuck in an incessant loop about the past or future. Our children beg us to clear our minds and turn the dial to their channel. They will give us every bit of information we need to take care of them, if only we become receptive to it.

There is no more real time to experience this than at night with a baby. Their need is often: *Hold me, I need to feel safe close to you.*

Yet, while we rock them, we hear: *By four months, your child should sleep in their crib alone, on a hard mattress, on their back. The ceiling fan must be on, and you must offer a pacifier to reduce the risk of SID's. Don't create any sleep associations, and sneak out once they're in a deep sleep...*

We've been conditioned to ignore what we feel and only listen to what we've been taught. It doesn't matter if we've been taught by our mother or a world-renowned doctor—what they say should complement what you feel is true rather than make you feel sick, resistant, uncomfortable, anxious, etc. Your body will not lie to you if you are trying to work with information that it doesn't feel is authentic.

You know when your parents used to say, "This hurts me more than it hurts you?" Well hello, that is your first clue that what you're doing is WRONG. Right action FEELS right at a cellular level.

Actual love is a flawless guidance system. When you are whole and can feel love without need, dependency, or control, it will steer you in a morally correct direction, always. Sorry King James, but when you are tuned in to that highest energy of your Being, you certainly don't need a book to point out right from wrong. You will clearly feel what is right, what is moral, what is loving, and what has reverence for the energy of life itself.

We are continually informing others and the universe of what we want through our energy. We are receiving in life from the channel we are tuned to: fear or love. The good stuff, the fantastic stuff, the, *I can't believe this is my life,* stuff comes only when we stop resisting life and tune into love.

Changing Patterns and Setting Boundaries

First, we stop reacting (and start meditating/ self-care daily)

Then we stop acquiescing

Then we stop partaking in any judgment (most of the time)

Then we do/say what we really want to do/say

Ignore their tantrum, hold the boundary (let them know what behavior we won't tolerate by moving away from any that is unacceptable)

Stop enabling, ignore another tantrum, hold the boundary

Then we stay in a state of love

Then we treat ourselves like we love ourselves

Still ignoring tantrums but wrapping the person in love and offering empathy, while holding the boundary

Tantrums slow, then stop

Drama is met with silence and burns out

They rise up (slowly)... or move out of our lives
Either way, it serves both of us

Authentic Action Step #5:

From today forward, every time you're faced with a choice, do what YOU want to do, and feel is right, without guilt. Physically move away from words & behavior that doesn't reflect your worth.

"How you're speaking to me is unacceptable."

Chapter 6: *Mirror, Mirror, One and All*

It's our desire to either deal with something later or not acknowledge it at all that gets us in trouble in the present. Because of the way we have been conditioned, we've trained ourselves to live, in our minds, anywhere but the present moment. The present moment is an inconvenience along the way to some better moment in our heads. For some reason, we think this makes us more successful. We fail to see how worrying about the next 15 things we have to do while we do the current one means we'll be less successful. Success is not someplace you arrive someday, just like happiness isn't. Both are something you can only experience right now, at this very moment. Right now, you are reading a book about marriage, possibly learning new ideas about what it means for you and your personal growth. If you were reading this book and thinking about your kids and the laundry and the dirty dishes, then you are not going to have any insights from it at all. You might read five paragraphs and not hear a single word.

Life asks us to have that same presence at every moment. Especially with our kids, especially with others, and especially in the way we share our gifts with the world. It asks us to stop making up stories about the future and the past and living in those places, which indeed do not exist. We cannot control either. We have no power in them. As Eckhart Tolle says, we only have power right NOW. In THIS moment. We must learn to mind our thoughts, so we don't waste year after year living mindlessly, going through the motions but never truly experiencing each breath.

Pull the Thorns

So, if at this moment you feel uneasy about something that is being said or done, then it has touched on something within you that your soul desires to heal. Rather than judging the situation, or the person, ask why. What is this here to teach me? How is this serving me? What forgotten part of me needs to be remembered? Have I failed to set needed boundaries? Have I failed to take care of myself and have my needs met? Do I have a habit of wasting time and making myself rush through activities? Have I been avoiding tasks and procrastinating? Have I been distracting myself with mindless activities rather than just focusing on how I can be successful in each moment?

Michael A. Singer, the author of *The Untethered Soul*, calls these moments of upset thorns. Do you know how, if you touch a cactus, no matter how hard you try to get all of the thorns out there will still be one that you can't see that only hurts when you touch the skin in just the right spot? That's what these are—old thorns we've stuffed down and tried to forget exist—pain we've "toughed out" and "moved on" from. And when we go to examine the fear they represent, we'll find it's rooted either in something that happened to us in childhood or beliefs from culture that don't serve us. The Shoulds of life. *You should go to church, you should get a college education, you should stay home with your kids, you should get married, you should do your homework, you should lose weight.* We call that the BS of life - our Belief Systems. We have hundreds of them and rarely do they serve us at all. Most are fear and lack based. The belief that you are unworthy of doing what you want is a false belief that needs to be changed. Moving into a new belief, perhaps just "I'm worthy" instead of "I'm not worthy," is vital for our success. When we take action from the place of "I'm worthy," we are living in a state of Love. And only in this state will life unfold for us in a meaningful, beautiful way.

Our emotions are our soul's GPS system, and when we feel the positive energy from them, we are happy, and usually don't think too much about the situation. But when we feel something more negative, we start to look around to blame who is causing us to be unhappy. We need to shift that focus to, *"What am I doing that is not authentic? How am I not trusting myself? What does this remind me of?"* Our soul desires us to be happy and to be successful, and it will point out anything that is in contrast to the life we envisioned for ourselves before we even were born.

We fear change as much as we desire happiness at the end of the day. Having the courage to make changes comes from moment-by-moment acts of bravery to identify and transform what is no longer serving us.

The thorns from childhood events are buried under layers of pain from those and similar circumstances. For example, I have a memory from my fourth birthday party of my brother leading all the guests through the house and telling me I couldn't play with any of them. That feeling of rejection has followed me the rest of my life, from people at school, to co-workers, to people I know and love from classes we take together. Even when others aren't actually rejecting me, I've often created a story in my head where they are. Just feeling confident walking into a room feels like an internal battle between the reality of the situation and the antique beliefs cluttering my psyche. Recently, I realized that the rejection story didn't even start with my birthday party—it started before that, with my mother.

I've had clients recall one specific event with a sibling where they did something innocent which harmed the sibling, and the parent reacted with fear, shaming them. Just one event—five minutes frozen in time—that follows them forty years later. Or a client yelled at as a child, told that they should do more activities at school, get better grades, or clean their rooms. These moments where we feel rejected and unloved, unworthy of love, create walls around our hearts. Honestly, it's practically impossible to raise a child without these events. Even if you don't do something unconscious, someone in their lives will. We'll all carry "stuff" with us from somewhere. Introspection and reflection and deconstructing to find the origin of these limiting beliefs are not to cast blame or shame on the people involved in creating them. I don't carry any ill-will toward my mother, brother, or my family. It's not about that. They were just passing on what happened to them. It's about becoming the best version of me now, and that means unpacking this emotional baggage I've been hauling around for over three decades.

Co-Creation

It is far easier for us to immediately blame others for our stress response than it is to just acknowledge our role in the co-creation of the event. The other morning I was gone a little bit longer than usual dropping the kids off to school. I'd left both of our dogs out, even though the older one has a tendency to scrounge for food. Many a loaf of bread has been lost to this dog. The other dog won't do anything like this, so we usually leave her out while putting the older one in her kennel when we leave. That morning it didn't dawn on me that there would be a need to.

I came home to find the kitchen floor under a blanket of papers, wrappers, and other assorted rubbish. I looked up and remembered that I'd gathered up the trash and had LEFT THE BAG ON THE KITCHEN CHAIR. In my mind when I did it, I'm sure I just thought I'd fill it up later and then toss it in the trash bin outside, forgetting about the dogs can get into unsupervised.

While the gut reaction was to be mad at the dog, i quickly reminded myself that I SHOULD have just thrown the trash out, why on earth would I just leave it on the chair really? Am I that cheap that I can't find another trash bag later, or just go finish filling it up then and be done with it?

Deeper still, I have a tendency to leave projects incomplete, to be interested in a million things, start all of them, and walk away before they are finished. This was a small branch of a much larger tree, yet another mirror reminding me of areas I have left to improve.

Yesterday, my husband noticed a pile of brewed K-Cups just sitting in front of the Keurig machine and actually picked them up to throw them away. I'm sure he thought he just earned brownie points, but I quickly started to lament that I was saving those to put the coffee grounds on the new houseplants, something I'd remembered can be beneficial and wanted to try.

He continued to throw them out anyway and told me if I really wanted them to go get them back out. But my role in this was that I had just left them on the counter like trash instead of collecting them or even just using them right away. In my mind, I thought, well I'll add them to the plants on Saturday when I water. I'll deal with that later. I didn't think I needed to communicate that with him because he's almost never, ever noticed anything to be picked up or thrown out!

Identifying the Mirror

I think the single most profound lesson I've learned so far on this entire path of awakening to a more conscious life is this: Everything another person does that bothers me, is about me, and I've almost always been partially responsible for creating it. That means taking full ownership of our powerful role as a co-creator in every moment of our lives. Who wants to do that?? In our minds, it's far easier to point the finger at others than to accept responsibility for even a fleeting minute of our own unhappiness. But the fact is, this contrast of seeing what we don't want, allows us to uncover what we do want—both in others and in ourselves. Let me share some examples.

Before I do, know the key to deconstructing is to find the fear or unmet need behind the behavior. It helps to ask questions like:

- **What am I afraid of right now that this person is shining a light on?**
- **What are they doing that reminds me of something I do that I'm unhappy with or something that happened in my life before?**
- **What thoughts are running through my head when this happens?**
- **How is this moment serving me and my growth?**
- **What belief am I believing about myself that is so untrue that my soul is generating an emotion of pain right now?**
- **What conditioned belief, from my parents or culture, am I wrongly believing to be true right now?**

Let's say there's a man on your social media and every time you see his posts or comments, you just want to block him, they annoy you so much. You start to think about them more - why don't you like them? Well, maybe they seem judgmental, robotic, lacking any empathy or vulnerability. You ask, am I doing this? You think back to a time someone called you condescending or told you to get off your high horse, or accused you of talking down to them. At the time, you thought it was just their problem, and they weren't ready for your wisdom, but now, sitting in front of the mirror, you realize you have a lot in common with this person that rubs you the wrong way. You vow to work on your delivery; being more vulnerable, more empathetic, more humble. Maybe just the way you word things needs to be tweaked. Perhaps you jump to the solution without acknowledging the problem or relating that you've been there and you understand how it might be feeling for them. Perhaps you need to just hold the space for them to share without offering your perceived wisdom. Or maybe that's not the case, but you know him well, and you see inauthenticity in his posts. Rather than judging him, ask where YOU are inauthentic in your own life? What are you doing that is in contrast to the way you talk or teach? Or maybe he reminds you of your mother or someone else from your childhood, and you need to go back and do some inner child healing, giving yourself what adults didn't give you then. Re-parenting yourself.

Another example, this time involving road rage: You aren't running late to work, of course, because you have exactly the 15 minutes you need to get to the office right on time, which you've carefully calculated. However, Slow-Mc-Slow-Pants has just pulled out in front of you and is crawling ahead at five under the speed limit. Your blood starts to boil. As if he can predict your route, he makes all of the same turns in front of you, stopping at every yellow light, blocking the left lane so you can't pass. Obscenities leave your mouth as you yell directions at him. Then you ask, what am I afraid of? Well, you're fearful of not getting to work on time and losing your job. What are they doing that reminds me of something I do that I'm unhappy with? Perhaps you're annoyed with yourself that your morning isn't more organized and that you hit the snooze button three times, so you're at the very limit of leaving with enough time to get to work. You've been so focused on the destination that you weren't present throughout the morning and have been in a constant state of rushing since your feet hit the floor. You might even be angry that you're going to this job again—you clearly aren't happy there, and perhaps it's time to make a change. Your soul is asking you to reevaluate this part of your life so you can create exactly what you do want.

Or your spouse leaves all of the cupboard doors open when he's in the kitchen. It drives you mad to look at all your dishes just hanging out in the open and know you have to go shut the doors AGAIN, for like the millionth time. You ask, what am I afraid of? You might be fearful of having to do everything for everyone else so often that you get no time for yourself. You ask what does this remind me of? Perhaps you are leaving projects unfinished, tasks incomplete, leaving areas of your life in chaos where others have to pick up the slack. How is this serving me? Maybe you need to enable less, allow others to be as capable as they truly are, take more time for yourself, or be present in your own work so that you aren't leaving things unfinished.

Maybe you can't stand to hear other people chewing their food, breathing loudly, or even humming. Your mind is consumed with wanting them to stop. You turn the TV up so you can't hear them, your legs twitching with irritation. You ask, what am I afraid of? And then you remember your own parents yelling at anyone that made noise during a meal, was a loud breather, or otherwise disrupted the supposed silence. You remember your father's reaction to it, the yelling or shaming that happened. It's become part of your programming, this subconscious reaction of fear to any noises that would have surely been noticed and corrected in your own childhood. In this case, you would need to remove the association you have with the sound. Or perhaps you are unhappy with your personal disruption of the silence… maybe you are afraid to use your voice, create, be imperfect, or be the center of attention. Or you dislike that you are unwilling to listen to others. You want to be listened to, heard, and seen for who it is you are. It bothers you that it's so hard for you to hold space for others' feelings or emotions, seeing their raw, real selves, but your pain is too great to allow this. Perhaps you have been lacking taking time for self-care, and you just do not have the space for this disruption of what you thought was about to be an act of self-care for you. Or, it bothers you that the other person is so unafraid to be who they are, and you have been pretending to be someone else to fit in your whole life.

If you harshly judge others for doing "stupid" things, it probably means you were harshly judged the same way when you were a child and continue to harshly judge yourself now. You may never feel like you are enough as you are, striving for some fictitious level of "perfection."

If I'm annoyed by someone's poor work ethic, it's worth looking at my own. Did I even stop to see the divine in this customer service rep before I demanded he fix the problem with my bill? Did I genuinely see him first? Do I truly see myself? Did I create the situation myself that I'm upset with them for?

Someone posted online that she is triggered when her husband leaves the house with dry skin on his face. When I pressed her about why this might bother her, in her mind it was all about him: *He needs to take care of his skin. He needs to make an effort to look nice. He needs to want to look nice when he's with me.* Maybe that is so, but this is not why it BOTHERS her. Where are those judgments coming from? Where is that fear coming from? I am willing to bet that no one but her has ever noticed his dry skin. If she looks deeper, perhaps she'll find that it's a mirror of her own neglect of self, ultimately respect for self and feelings of worthiness. She may feel he doesn't respect her or find her worthy because he's not taking care of himself, in this minor way or in even bigger ways that could affect his health. Perhaps her own seeming lack of time for self-care, for doing things for herself to refill and refuel are also in the mirror. It doesn't necessarily mean it's something physical that bothers her; maybe she's not showing up 100% in her job or her other roles. Somewhere, there is a hidden fear that she hasn't tapped into. It's not really about him other than a possible worry about how he will be able to show up for her in the future. I'm unable to come up with any way dry skin has a real negative impact on her life - it does not cost her anything by way of preventing her from saying yes to something she does want. She doesn't have to say no to anything to say yes to this.

Likewise, when we get mad with our child for taking so long to get dressed - it's not the fact that they are slow that actually bothers us. It's our fear about where we have to be and getting there on time. Or it's the fact that this is inconvenient and preventing us from doing something for ourselves that we would rather be doing than watching them twirl around the flying underwear when they're supposed to be getting dressed. At bedtime, our cups are depleted, and we are desperate to go refill them. We've spent energy thinking all day, doing physical labor, working our jobs, etc., and our fuel tank is totally empty. They're in fear because bedtime means goodbye and we spend the entire day convincing them they need us for everything. Last night I even said to my daughter, "I'm running on empty. I'm tired, and I need to sleep. I really, really need to just go to bed right now, so I'm sorry if I'm grumpy with you. It has nothing to do with you, I'm just wiped out and need to go lay down. What could we do so I can go to sleep and you can feel safe?"

Why Awakening is Easier with Our Children

Having your own child is the ultimate path to growth, and this is why I feel so strongly about Conscious Parenting and shifting the entire parenting dynamic. We wouldn't need to even discuss Conscious Parenting if people stopped having babies until they were in a whole place and fully ready for the weight of that responsibility. If they were fully in a place of self-acceptance where they refused to dump their own stuff on their child, and instead could see their child's needs without filters of their own lack, no one would need to learn how to be present. However, in my case, it hasn't been my children that trigger me (yet). I remember when it finally dawned on me that my children weren't going to be what launched me into growth, but rather my husband was—still this new awareness was brought on by their arrival. The idea of applying everything I knew about Conscious Parenting to him was foreign to me. It was like I'd put all of the teachings in a little box and still held him to some outrageous expectations to consistently make me happy and fall in line.

When it comes to adults, we rightly view them as responsible to fix their own shit. We may consider our relationships with them as disposable. Unfortunately, we don't realize that whatever dynamic we held with them, we will hold with someone else. Even the partner that seemed perfect before we were married WILL become our mirror and hold up a reflection of the unhealed parts of ourselves once those parts feel safe to surface.

Just last evening I was discussing an experience my husband had with another man that plays a video game with him. These people play together every night, with strategy sessions and even their fair share of drama. It's his community, and it's authentic to him, just like I have a large supportive community online from my classes as well.

Anyway, he had a problem with an older man that had a problem with everyone else. As he described the scenario to me, I realized this relationship was a very near replica of that with his father. He was being tasked again with healing that dynamic.

Life is Like a Funhouse

There may be multiple reflections in the mirror others hold up to us. They may remind us of a part of us we've lost. They show us where we fail to love ourselves. They may remind us of our parents, good or bad. They may remind us of something we're afraid of or wish we could stop doing. But the fact is, any time we have a reaction to what another is doing, it means they are no longer reflecting the best parts of ourselves, they are now reflecting something about us we don't like for whatever reason, and that is a GIFT. They are reflecting something that is incomplete.

You might be wondering, what on earth do you mean that's a gift? But that is indeed The Gift. It's the whole point and purpose of coming to this Earth, whether you believe in reincarnation or not. That is, spiritual evolution THROUGH relationships: growth to become a whole being that is aligned with our soul which, at its very core, is Love. Without these interactions, we would be safe in our bubble, in our mirror-less room, where we could remain in a comfortable state of stagnancy.

Even those that follow a spiritual path and believe they have done nothing but self-improvement and healing for the majority of their life, for decades even, but have mostly remained in uncommitted relationships, are not allowing the catalyst for true EMBODIMENT of the growth. This is called Spiritual Bypass. It is one thing to be fully present and aware when you are sitting alone in a room. It is an entirely other thing to be fully present and aware while a toddler or your husband is tantrumming. **Relationships, the muck of them, again, are the true path to spiritual awakening.**

Each encounter, from the cashier at the grocery store to the man driving slow in front of us, is designed to lead us closer to our truth. There are no accidental meetings. Each human being in your life serves this purpose if you allow them. Some will be your direct teachers, and some will just annoy the truth out of you.

This is a boring way to live sometimes, I'm telling you! There is no drama when you remove judgment from your life or realize that judgment for another is actually a judgment you hold for yourself.

For example, I have a female client who now recognizes when her sister is judging others. In the past, she may have joined in the conversation, even may have been entertained by the gossip. Now it's just kind of annoying.

Learning from the light others shine on your wounds just takes getting curious. When I got really curious about why I had a dynamic with girl friends that kept repeating, where they seemed to get very critical out of nowhere and the relationship would either implode or we'd just quietly go our separate ways, I had the major realization that I was projecting the dynamic I've had with my mother on all of these woman-woman friendships! I would become the child that wasn't seen and they would become the critical mother, finding any flaw they could and poking holes in my confidence. To shine my full light, to be authentic, would mean revealing that I had wisdom greater than their own present awareness, and I was terrified to hurt them with it. My wisdom had been shut down early, and I remembered the pain and just kept playing it out, for the past three decades of my life!

This is why marriage can be looked at as a blessing if you choose this path on purpose: being stuck with someone at least until the time that you are aware of the growing you have yet to do means you can often see the lesson much faster. Whether you decide to stay committed and let your partner be the teacher is up to you. If you leave, another teacher will arrive. If you allow them to align to the vision your soul wishes to create, then there is no need to find a new teacher. If they refuse to meet you in that vision, then you may end up moving on.

With children, on the other hand, the commitment is non-negotiable (usually). They arrive and their very survival depends on you. The imprint they will leave on the world depends, in large part, on how you raise them and what you show them about life and Love. They are learning everything from what you model. From the way they keep their house to the kinds of partners they marry, you are often an unknowing designer of their future.

That's why it's ironic that we view it as our task to teach them all of these things and control them into submission to our will, when the fact of the matter is that nothing we tell them to do as a parent sticks but everything we actually do is cemented. Even if you were raised by abusive parents but are not an abusive parent, you are still dealing with the voices in your head of shame and blame. You are likely attracting abusive partners and struggling to feel worthy because that's what they taught you. You were shown you weren't enough, so therefore you go through life still believing you aren't enough. Whatever we believe about ourselves is what we attract into our lives. This is true with money, circumstances, and relationships.

Authentic Action Step #6:

Remember the last time you thought about a person in your life on repeat (they just kept popping into your awareness). Get super curious about *why* whatever they did or said **REALLY** bothers you. Keep asking yourself *what else* until you feel you've traced it to the very root of the upset.

Chapter 7: *Practical Matters*

Fortunately, by the time I met my husband, I knew to at least discuss some of the big things with him. *What do you think about politics? What do you think about religion? How do you feel about kids? About pets?*

It didn't even dawn on me to say: *How will we manage housework? What are your spending habits like? If you walk past a full trash can, what do you do? How do you feel about vehicle maintenance? When would you be willing to move to another state? What would you do if I got a job in Hawaii?*

It sounds silly, but it's not only a meaningful conversation, it really is a common-sense conversation you should have before signing a contract to supposedly live with someone for the rest of your life.

As an empath, of course I gave him the wrong idea about who I was in the beginning. I would clean the house, or cook a meal, or do all his laundry. I felt I had to do those things to be desirable and receive love. If I were in my truth, those things weren't who I was. I mean, prior to kids I did try to keep them up, but they weren't in my core habits. They didn't come easily to me. I definitely wasn't a neat-freak minimalist or anything. I had plenty of worth issues and some mild hoarding tendencies. I had no awareness of the concept that doing those things is what loving oneself looks like because I had no awareness of even loving myself.

With him, I overlooked everything. Small warning signs weren't warning signs to me at all because I turned a blind eye to them, knowing my own side of the street wasn't clean and that he was a major step up in comparison to previous relationships.

In reality, we had a lot of the same issues. He liked his house clean but wasn't willing or able to do much about it - same here. He freely spent money and had lots of interests - same here.

But we also had some conflicting wants and values: I want to live where it's warm, he doesn't like the discomfort of moving and could care less about being in the heat. I want to keep growing and expanding, and like taking risks as an entrepreneur, he is happy at his 9-5. I want to invest and build assets - he just wants to keep acquiring more Ducati's. I'm very generous and love helping others, often financially, and he is less inclined to. One of our first arguments was about what we would do with the money if we suddenly became millionaires. He didn't want to give a dime away to hardly anyone other than close friends and I was already building a foundation with it. It was a hypothetical situation but was worth exploring as it actually identified areas where we both had a story that was limiting us.

Authentically You

To be able to ask these questions, you need to trust yourself enough to know what you truly value. I remember it took several years of dating guys and feigning interest in their activities before I realized that wasn't serving anyone and I needed to just be true to who I am and what I enjoy doing.

In this relationship, he loves to ride his motorcycle. I used to enjoy riding with him some (though clearly not on long trips), but then when the kids came, of course, that stopped.

I love swimming in a way I can't even describe (I think I'm actually part dolphin) and he doesn't even know how to swim. I want to go on tropical vacations, and that's the last thing he wants to do.

When it came to kids, I really thought I carefully vetted him there. He seemed great with kids and loved them. I was confident that he'd be a great dad. But when it came to actual child rearing, we didn't discuss the nitty-gritty. Fortunately, when I laid down the law early on that our children would never be punished, he was receptive. As I've immersed myself in the world of conscious parenting and child development, he's learned through osmosis along the way. But what if he didn't?

I see this complaint all of the time: *I'm conscious/peaceful/gentle, but their dad isn't... what do I do?* Can you imagine doing everything in your power to raise your child what you consider the right way, only to walk in the door to their mom or dad shaming or belittling them?

I didn't ask him if he'd be up in the night when they cried, if he'd gladly change diapers, how he felt about spending money on them, or any of the everyday stuff that easily causes fighting once the kids arrive.

And truth be told, I find almost everything else to be negotiable. Those are wants. Not getting to go to Playa Del Carmen with him is not going to trigger me. Having someone do something with my child that I have a strong reaction to? Now that is unreal. Our children, or how they are treated, will trigger us like no other.

My husband has a hard time with consent and bodily autonomy. He loves to be physically affectionate, tickling and tossing and hugging and kissing. It is one of the things I loved about him when we met, remember? Well, the kids will laugh AND say "No!" at the same time when he's playing with them, and it used to send me into high alert. I always want them to be listened to, and it's critical to me that they learn that their "No!" should be respected. So when this happens, I'm ready to lose my shit.

Often, they are having a ball and go back for more, and it was only me that had any anxiety about the situation. But the times I do need to stop it, it wasn't a simple "This is unacceptable, she said no." No, of course not, my default until recently had been to cross into raving lunatic territory. I didn't realize I needed to physically step in and remove them, but without the fear and the reality TV-esque reaction.

If you take differing ideas about child-rearing + addictions + different wants/values + terrible communication skills + empathic/narcissist personalities—the concept of divorce suddenly seems entirely plausible. Not only is it plausible, but it also begins to look desirable.

Values and Environments

I remember when I first saw my future husband's house. He had one of those giant Asian fans on his wall, and I was not a fan. Below, he had stacks of video games and movies, and in another room had rows of dusty collected model cars. *Whatever*, I thought, *he's a man and men have weird tastes. I've seen worse.* Little did I know we would eventually build a house together and I'd be fighting with him over those tastes (and longing to throw away all of it).

He probably remembers the first time he picked me up for a date. I think I had about eight different paint colors all within twenty feet of the front door. My TV was smaller than this laptop screen. And I had one giant dog (a Great Dane) leaping from loveseat to couch, drooling all over the place and crashing into him for snuggles.

These days, as a family of four, though he rarely says anything, there is this constant undertone in the house, this recognition that there is far too much clutter and mess, but the awareness that neither of us really know how to permanently change it. We have two young children, and the second you pick up one thing, five more take its place.

But it's not just the children. As I mentioned, most of the time (especially up until recently) only one of us (me) does any of the housework. That's unfortunate because I was raised for the most part in a household that didn't seem to have a mindset of even being worthy of living in a tidy house. We mostly cleaned for company. We did big cleaning maybe once a month, a few times a year, something like that. At any rate, it wasn't a daily thing. Which means that company ultimately was worthy of a tidy environment, but for some reason, we weren't. Practically, I know that this was because of time and available energy, failure to hold boundaries, etc. We swung from one extreme to the other rather than finding balance in keeping a tidy environment. It wasn't a boundary that was modeled consistently during those prime programming years, evidently.

When we did clean, it wasn't pleasant. There was anger and yelling, and it felt like a huge burden. I was hit with a belt once for growing tired from the endless trips to take one thing at a time up to where it belonged and my mom's subsequent discovery that I'd just started putting EVERYTHING she'd handed me in the toy box downstairs. I honestly don't know if the condition of the house was different before my parent's divorce or not, though I suspect it was. My dad was more involved with housework. When I'm around him now, I'm guaranteed to see him empty trash somewhere even if we're only going to be together for a few hours! He is on top of yard work and meticulous about his belongings. He likes things in their place and clean. He once scrubbed the graphics right off my stove top—my newer appliances are obviously not built to the same standards as those he grew up with.

If you were to enter my father's childhood home, I believe you'd see his mom and dad keeping their house spotless, with everything in its place. They also had six children so money was tight and there were just fewer things, in general, to care for. I imagine it was both essential and easy to care for what they did have, though the lack mentality—there's not enough or might not be enough for everyone—seems to have been firmly in place.

My mom, on the other hand, moved a lot as a child. She had less stability and a mother that never seemed to care much about housework but did care about appearances, with the judgment of others a core theme. I don't know much about their money situation, but I believe it was reasonably abundant, and she didn't want for much, spending a lot of time with her extended family. Her mother was more carefree and artistic, and they loved and kept animals. Her father was mostly absent, an alcoholic professional baseball player that was on the road or in warmer locales during the time he played.

In my husband's home, his mother did all of the housework and kept their house spotless. She picked up after him and made his bed and cooked all of the meals. She also managed their business, and his dad was a used car salesman and traveled buying cars to flip and sell. My husband never wanted for anything most of his childhood, and in fact, his father would buy him things all of the time, likely both his way of showing love and attempting to control.

You can imagine where I'm going with this. We have conflicting beliefs about several things: housework, money, décor, etc.

The following eight sections were channeled during a journaling session, and I have left it unedited for the most part. As I'm doing the final edits of the book, I realize that I have fully integrated almost all of these teachings in my life now, but when I started this book six months ago, these were areas I still greatly struggled in, so I asked my higher self for help.

Material Things

We place substantial energetic burdens on ourselves by wanting and obtaining material things. Currently, I have three stories of a house to maintain that we built around the dimensions of our huge pool table and master suite ensemble. I have two little kids, so I have bin after bin of toys and books. Dressers are overflowing with clothes—if they actually make it there after the laundry. All of these burdens comprise the fights we have: money, chores, laundry....

These things do not matter. They resolve themselves when each person makes a commitment to be more whole and more responsible. As each person lets go of their extremes: addictions, tendency to hoard, and insecurities, they will naturally be more easily manageable. When we rest in the middle rather than in excess or deficiency, our lives eventually match that state of balance.

As each person grows in the scope of love, they will have a new reverence for their belongings and their space, and these ideas of chores and to-do lists will be no longer needed.

If each person in a relationship takes these steps towards being whole, they will no longer feel any lack or overwhelm about their duties within the house in this form.

So within, will be without. They must start with their own personal form, their body, and then they can move outward to having the reverence for the space that they reside within.

See, it isn't so much that there's too heavy of a burden with the maintenance of whatever homestead and life we've chosen, as there is an unwillingness to be present in each moment and revere all things within it, to hold them sacred.

If you look at a dirty dish as a burden to move into the dishwasher rather than rotting food interfering with the vibration of your sacred space and belongings, you'll be less inclined to take care of it. Like all things, if you see it as a chore and obligation and doing it is "good" and not doing it is "bad," then you fail to SEE. You fail to open your eyes and delight in the food you've eaten or the beauty of the dish that it was served on. You've been unable to feel the embrace of the space you live within, of being grateful for its four walls, warmth, and light. You have stepped outside of your world and into your mind, and living in the mind is failing to live at all. Deep within your brain are the processes which allow you to realize and run from actual danger.

You are no longer running from tigers or avoiding snakes. You live in boxes and watch those dangers on another box from the comfort of your recliner. You no longer, typically, face any real situations where you need to be afraid on a daily basis. Therefore, your mind has resorted to making up things to be fearful of. Your culture has given you plenty, and the worst of all came from your religion, the fear of being "bad." Of being not good enough. Of being unlovable or unworthy.

So when we live in this place of fear rather than in a place of love, we fail to love everything around us. And that is when we go into survival mode and the chores of maintaining our sacred space, even of maintaining our sacred bodies, get morphed in our minds into existing within this fear. We live in Scare City—or scarcity—lack. Never enough to have or to eat, never good enough to deserve it, not enough for everyone, powerless to change our circumstances.

The stress is just too much—we check out. We scroll Facebook or play video games or watch TV. We check the heck out, lock the doors to our mind, and pretend we no longer exist in this scary place. We are so afraid of pain that we refuse to face it.... Yet the irony is that we have created the pain, all between our ears. We have assigned storylines to every aspect of our day rather than revere the amazing life within it. We replace gratitude for our belongings with fear about caring for them. We continue to buy, buy, buy until we are swimming in things, unable to even see the room that is holding us safe in its protective structure. We are surrounded by too much, scrolling Amazon for something more. *This Instapot will make me happy* - we decide - *as I can just throw frozen chicken and broth in and it will be done in twenty minutes.* That will give me SO MUCH TIME to…. To what? To watch TV? To look for something else to buy? To wish the kids were asleep so we could recline back and do nothing?

We have overwhelmed our space with doing, and we just keep creating more and more of it. We work too long for fear of not having money. We enroll our kids in every activity imaginable for fear they won't be successful without them. We try to cook elaborate meals for fear that just eating an apple or having a cup of nuts wouldn't be good enough.

Judgment, loud and reverberating from our pulpits and our culture deafens our ears, removes our ability to listen to the chorus of nature outside of our window. We are so busy judging ourselves and others as good or bad that we don't even look at what we are. We try to gain spiritual respite through this place called church and instead leave with a whole new set of reasons why we should be fearful or shrink into our not-good-enoughness.

It is madness! We have sold our soul for synthetic bliss that arrives in brown boxes from Amazon Prime (and nothing against Prime, I love it), unwilling to for even ONE brief moment feel our pain, awaken to our hurt, and heal ourselves to unleash our higher potential.

We are playing small. We are shrinking, donut by donut, trend by trend, degree by degree, until we fit into the masses and disappear. We are terrified of being big. We are mortified by the idea of brilliantly shining in our own light. We want approval, we want love, we want validation. Someone to tell us we are good enough! Please tell me I belong here and you love me! We create suffocating stress, and it manifests in our physical surroundings.

Love yourself, release your things, and continually reevaluate and change your outer space to match your inner space.

Money

When it comes to money, the flow of abundance matches the energy that is output by each person. Therefore, if one person is not putting any energy out but only receiving, then the balance of money will not equal. Each person in a relationship needs to devote time to giving of themselves. They will also then be in a place where they can receive. If each partner is matched in this respect, then there will be no animosity or hoarding of money.

Whatever feeling you have when money is abundant is the feeling you must always maintain to keep it. It is living in your truth, your authentic and aligned state, that allows this to happen.

You must drop any hidden beliefs about money, any hidden blocks you've created by deeming yourself unworthy to receive it. Treat it as another precious relationship in your life here to awaken you to wholeness. Have respect for it and take action to create it when needed. With each chance to spend it, ask yourself what the loving choice would be.

Sex

Sex is an energy exchange. Again, if each person is whole than there will be no imbalance. If no one is feeling lack, then there will be no pressure to fill a void with sex. If each person is feeling abundant, then they will gladly meet together to blend their energies like paint on canvas, coloring the energy of the relationship into vibrant colors and states of bliss. This isn't about a lack-based activity; sex originally was intended as a way to create an energy that closely resembles God/Source energy, we can also call it Love. It is to fill the home with this energy of Love. It is not dirty nor secret. This act is a joining of souls that otherwise can only be felt outside of the body in other dimensions, what you may call heaven. At orgasm, you will feel the bliss that is your true nature. You can also reach this place on your own, by revisiting your own soul. Your energy comes in from the area of your genitals, near where your original eight cells remain, and when you keep pulling that energy into those cells and invite it without resistance, you experience bliss again. Read more about sex in Chapter 9.

Kids

Taking care of the kids isn't an issue unless one person is not whole. They will not feel stress or strain by these activities unless they have not demanded the time they need to love and care for themselves. When they are abundant in this space, these duties no longer feel like duties, but like divine interactions with spirit. Children are very close to source, and this energy exchange with a child is often a mirror adults in pain are unwilling to face. If you have a spouse that is strongly resistant to caring for a child, it means they cannot bear to withstand the reflection of how far they have come from source energy. They are longing to be whole but unwilling or unknowing how to get there. Therefore, each person must share their desires as to what they need to care for themselves. They may need to get help from the outside, such as daycare or a nanny or housekeeper, in order to find that time that they need to recharge, refuel, and create. Children benefit from knowing many and loving many, therefore do not hesitate to allow them to be amongst their peers and loving caregivers that meet their needs. They know this as natural, though they are attached to you when you are present. They will also tap into their own reservoirs of wholeness when in this state without any attachments of fear energy left by you.

Chores

We don't have a division of labor problem in marriage, we have a blindness to our divine light, though it is always there. We don't have a lazy husband, we have two people that are unwilling to face their fears and evolve. If we did, we would begin to give away. We would have fewer toys to pick up. We would have fewer clothes to wash. We would have more than enough time to lovingly sweep the floors we are grateful for, to shine them as though they were new. We would have more than enough time to carry our plates to the dishwasher and return the table to its perfectly empty state. We would be overflowing with time to manage our laundry or pick up our cars.

As it is, this growth takes a while. It is not an overnight process to reverse this habitual way of thinking and living. There are ways to begin to take action. You can outsource housework. You can outsource accounting. You can buy a robotic vacuum and run it every day, realizing it only takes five minutes or so to pick up so it can run. You can empty the trash, wash the dishes, and launder your clothes daily - realizing that breaking it up makes the task much more manageable. You can break down the general cleaning over the course of the week, so you are only spending ten minutes a day scrubbing anything, or even cleaning up everything each day as you use it. Basically, you are avoiding extremes and living in balance.

But ultimately, you're going to have to stop wasting your time avoiding your pain and start lovingly caring for the things you own that you are grateful for, and releasing all of the things no longer serving you. I love the idea behind the popular "KonMari Method," where you hold each item and see if it still sparks joy for you, after having gathered every single one of those items in your home in one place so you can clearly see the excess you have.

I'm not saying we all have to live like minimalists. That is a much lower-stress way to live, of course, but it's not for everyone. You will continue to fill the lack in your lives through material belongings until you begin to fill it with love. You cannot overcome the feeling of stress until you take time daily to renew your being and enter the state of love and gratitude. Some people are more comfortable with clutter because it makes them feel loved and like there is an abundance of reminders that they are loved everywhere they look. They feel the energy within each item and collect all of that energy to keep around should they one day return to a state where they feel depleted. For them, it's not about the actual belongings, it's the way they inevitably do end up everywhere around them. That is their evidence that they are not alone and they are loved. If they can find this place within, then their without begins to match. Their rooms become more "bare" because their hearts are more full. They no longer need these energetic items to make them feel abundant. Their abundance comes from the heart and their connection to Source.

You will begin to make small changes, space by space, and eventually room by room. Go to a room and meditate in it until you feel the great power of tremendous Love that is within. When you open your eyes in this state, you will have no other want but to clear the space, or at least lovingly take care of what it is in it. You must do this process in the room itself, or your focus will not go there, you will not associate the room and its belongings with the feeling of abundance, especially if you are so early in the practice that it doesn't linger with you long after meditation. Start the meditation with the intention for the space to reflect your inner space, your authentic self, when you are done. Remember places and natural locations that you felt most at home in, and then seek to mirror those spaces within your home. Eventually, you should never turn a corner and feel outside of yourself. Your belongings and your internal space should blend so perfectly that another soul isn't able to discern where your form begins or ends.

For toys and the joyous spreading that children love to do, the parent should always relax and allow, but at the same time, not fill the space with toys from their own anxiety. They should keep each area clean for the child to explore and grow within. There is no need for toys. Children do not, on their own, need toys to learn. Of course, you find them fun and feel your kids will as well, but they actually hamper their natural abilities to play and explore. Look at how your children rarely play with their toys, but you just keep buying more. If you were to remove them all now, they would not be heartbroken, as you are likely anxious about them being. They should only have as many of their own belongings as they are capable of caring for—and the same advice goes for you. Whatever you can longingly keep, is what you should have. Anything else is too much.

Give away anything you don't need. If you need money, you can sell your belongings, but otherwise, give away and give away freely. As you release the energy back out into the universe for those that need it, you invite more energy to come into you in the new ways which you desire it. If you can help another at least feel more comfortable with the belongings you no longer need, why not do that? That is likely one of your values, it is a universal value actually, that we take care of one another and give when we can. Instead of thinking your bank account prevents you from giving, give of your belongings. You probably have far too many anyway. It is time for you to bless and release, and thank them for the way they served you up until this point. You no longer need them. Others will benefit from this blessing, as when they receive your belongings, they will also receive the loving energy that you have assigned to them. Care for them even in donation, do not just throw them in a bin.

Bills

Bills are part of your daily life, but they are your unwillingness to live any other way. Bills do not have to be so. You can live without them, though now it is very hard to be self-sufficient. Thus, whatever you put out you will receive. If you do not try to continue to take beyond what you are putting out, then you will not struggle with paying your bills. In cases where one partner tries to control the other with money, that partner has set themselves up as not feeling worthy of receiving. They are giving more than they receive. You must restore the balance within before it will reflect without. As soon as the partner begins to receive love in all forms, he or she will no longer feel controlled by money, and it will flow in his or her direction.

Food

Food in excess is also an expression of wanting to get energy rather than generate it on our own. Often in our culture now, we use food as this reason for connection or gathering. You do not need to do this. Food was intended for your use to fuel alone, not to love one another. You have perverted the use of food to take the place of the love that is within all of you. Cooking the food or creating recipes has its place in creative expression, but it is not necessary for food's intended purpose of fueling. For those that abuse and consume more food than they need, they will begin to see a cost for that behavior in their physical vessel. To overcome this, they must learn to both receive love from themselves and others and witness their own potential for energy creation, and they also must revere the food they do eat, so that it is not eaten blindly. We recommend that you do not follow these power-based controls of diets, but begin to eat food one by one, closer to its whole form, rather than putting an excessive amount of different foods on one plate because you can. When you are able, eat and enjoy one item of food, grateful for the energy it's allowing you to consume, thankful for the life it had before it was harvested, and grateful for your ability to be one with it. Feel the sensations in your body before, during, and after eating so, you can identify true hunger from eating out of anxiety and realize the pleasurable experience you are having. In this fashion, food will adequately nourish and fill you rather than lead you to want more and more.

Pets

Pets are divine beings that closely mimic Source energy in their complete absence of judgment. Many people keep pets because of this very reason. They sense their high vibrational energy and are restored by petting or watching them. Many people are overwhelmed by the care and keeping of a pet, because they, again, are asleep. They are failing to be present in their lives, and often pet owners have a great deal of past pain that they are unwilling to face. When a pet becomes a burden in the home, that is a sign that there is an overall failure to care for the self. Thus, there is limited energy to care for others. Pets need daily exercise and grooming, as well as a sacred space to call their own. They thrive in positive energy environments and begin to have odd behavior, such as separation anxiety or fear, in negative environments. If their owner is not whole, they will take on all of the inadequacies of the owner. They will have the same anxieties and fears and will be unable to relax. Pet owners may be so ripped open from their childhood wounds that they are unable to live without the calming energy of a pet. Therefore, if a partner desires a pet, take it as a sign that they may have some deep healing to do, if they are not already whole and very high vibration. The unconditional love of a pet can inspire not only healing, but growth and a giving nature the owner may not already possess. Therefore, it is a sacred task to care for and keep a pet. But like with all other things, having too many pets is an inadequacy in the owner and doesn't serve anyone. The animals long to be in their natural home or a loving environment that supports them to live a whole, healthy, and abundant life.

All other complaints are about addictions that both souls need to heal. You can invite them into your vision of wholeness, but you can't make them enter it. They must decide to do so when they are ready. If their incomplete nature does not allow you to enter your own vision of wholeness, and they are unwilling, then you must move on to a situation or relationship that does not prevent you from your personal growth.

Authentic Action Step #7:

Ask yourself what the loving choice would be—from you, to you— before any action you take today.

Chapter 8: *Pleasure*

Chasing pleasure… so many of us do it, especially if we had parents that didn't support us during our intense emotional experiences, who didn't mirror what we were feeling and let us know it was totally okay and understandable to be upset. Hence "emotional eating"—or anything else we do to cope when we're anxious or upset. Pleasure may have been denied—either due to religious reasons or simply not feeling like we had the money or ability to go do the things that gave us pleasure. What do you do that truly brings you joy? When do you feel in flow, enjoying every fleeting second of what you're doing?

For the vast majority of us, we find pleasure in all of the wrong places, driven by our ego's want of MORE. Craving is in overdrive while the motivation to be productive takes a backseat.

Addiction

Not all relationships will involve addiction, but some people may not even know there is an addiction at play. The knowledge that the brain registers ALL pleasures in the same way, and that we can become addicted to gambling, shopping, and sex, as well as drugs and alcohol is relatively recent. When we partake in the pleasurable activity, the brain releases the neurotransmitter dopamine. This function was initially intended for our survival—eating and having sex are imperative to make it as a species, so we needed to be motivated to partake. And initially, having this experience was a lot harder than it is today—now we get a quick boost of dopamine which ends up decreasing dopamine production in the long-term—leading to a craving for more. The process of addiction is a very intense wanting, seeking, or desire to have/do something that we then get increasingly less pleasure from.

ADHD is associated with having low levels of dopamine. Since dopamine is what motivates us and helps us feel rewarded for doing and accomplishing tasks, some of those with ADHD just aren't wired to be go-getters like dopamine-dominant people are.

Meditation, sleep, getting a massage, exercising, eating foods that are rich in tyrosine (tyrosine is a building block of dopamine—eggs, soy, bananas, beans, fish, almonds, avocados, chicken), and listening to certain music are all healthy ways to increase dopamine naturally.

I knew that I overeat, but it wasn't until very recently that I realized that I am addicted to food. I think addiction can be defined as any activity you do to escape your reality that seems outside of your control, or any behavior you continue to do despite its negative consequences. The word "addiction" comes from a Latin term for "enslaved by" or "bound to." The addiction is a buffer to pain. It is the habits that you may have an inner dialogue about, that you try to rationalize, where you can hear part of you saying to *just do it, you deserve it,* and another part saying *don't, this will hurt you,* or reminding you of its cost. It makes sense that most of us don't realize we have one as this is the first step to changing an addiction—acknowledging that it exists. Only then can we begin to understand the root cause of our behavior and take action to change it.

Because we have been taught that discomfort is bad and that we must avoid pain, in stress we turn to substances that soothe us or activities that allow us to go below thinking, so we no longer ruminate about what is bothering us. When the anxiety starts to rise, we turn to the habit like a young child to a pacifier. We need that hit of dopamine and serotonin to relax.

Eating actually turns off our stress response—our bodies are set up so they know we aren't in danger if we have time to eat. The fat from the excess food is stored close to our livers in our abdomen so it can be quickly utilized if there's another "threat."

If the person you are with is fighting an addiction, you must first know that the habit is theirs to heal. Only they can take the journey to release the enormous grief, pain, or shame that is causing the addictive behavior. You can neither wake them up to this nor fix it for them. The timing for them to acknowledge, uncover, and heal the reaction that causes this is perfect for their growth. You cannot move the time forward or backward. You can only refuse to enable these habits and stop any attempts to prevent them from the natural consequences of their actions.

However, if the addiction is preventing them from serving you (in the ways discussed earlier: see you, hear you, and honor your worth), if it truly costs you, then YOU must make a choice on what to do with the relationship. That may look like ending it, that may look like rediscovering your own worth and setting boundaries, and that may look like having your needs met elsewhere. There is no dictate that you stay with someone. In fact, you may prevent or delay their healing by staying with them and not allowing them to realize the full cost of their behavior. The action on your part must come from a space of love and knowing how it's affecting your own life, rather than trying to fix theirs. Unless the behavior affects your health or well-being (in other words, leave if they're abusive), I feel you should spend time in this new state of love, working on yourself, before making the decision to leave. Love does heal, and you may inspire them to love themselves through your own transformation.

When They're Grumpy

Likewise, if the stress that you are escaping through addiction is genuinely CAUSED by the other person, then you know you must change the relationship to end the pain-avoiding behavior you are partaking in. If you are doing everything you can to love yourself, to meet your needs, to raise your vibration, and know your worth, and still they treat you as less than worthy, then the relationship may no longer serve you. You may feel like a balloon floating through the clouds, perfectly happy and content. Then your husband comes in with a ton of fear, super grumpy, and it's as though he yanks the string tied to you and rips you out of the clouds down to his level. He wants you to be small, to only be seen by those on the ground with him. He wants to keep you at his level. You must decide if you will continue to wear the string around your neck or if you desire to cut the cord and float freely.

I've gotten stuck. Rather than allow myself to soar, I eat to literally weigh myself down to the ground with the negativity and low-frequency vibrations. I eat to camouflage myself, to dim myself, to shrink myself—shrink the number of people that can see me, ultimately, the number of people I can serve. Part of my food addiction is merely for protection, a suit of fat armor to make me invisible to the predators of my past. I've also read that the hug of the fat is to replace a missing embrace from one's mother. The voice that tells me to go ahead, eat it anyway, is at times a very frightened little girl who was yanked from the sky so early that she is terrified to fly, and at times a defiant teenager that responds to my attempts at personal boundaries the same way she did to her mother.

As I work to heal this, it is a slow process. It is hard to gain power over an addiction because it requires us to do our best to heal the negative voice and to make a new choice when we still hear it. Gary Zukav says that every time we make a conscious choice over the addictive behavior, we gain more power over it, and I find this to be true. However, thinking of this in terms of only the "conscious choice" still gives the feeling that there is a "good" choice and a "bad" choice, which can lead to shame and guilt. What I find to help me have true clarity is: Does this choice reflect my love for my Self? What would the loving option be right now? That takes everyone else and all judgment out of the equation.

Overeating may be the only addiction that others can really immediately associate you with. If you're addicted to sex or gambling or drinking, you may be able to easily hide that from most people. Thus overeating keeps men and women like me in a cycle of shame—shame for eating, shame for others seeing that we've eaten. We feel the pull to keep ourselves in that state because it is what we felt when we were young. Shame is the lowest frequency energetic state there is, so in the end, we often attract the lowest frequency vibrational people and situations into our life.

Because our close loved ones entrain to our energy, if we're in shame, they can end up there too. And our children inherit our shame if we don't make an effort to not pass on our own anxiety. That is some considerable motivation, probably the best, to overcome an addiction. Yet, it still feels like an uphill battle. We control it through abstinence and are happy for a while, and then something triggers its return. Is it genuinely possible to completely resolve an addiction? Of that, I'm not sure.

Those that experienced childhood abuse, especially sexual abuse, may eat to keep themselves in the state of shame they are used to. They might put food in their bodies without their true consent, reliving the experience of something entering or hurting their body without their permission as a child. They may wish to stay in this state of shame because the armor of fat camouflages them to others. Inside there is a little girl or boy that is absolutely terrified and ashamed and doesn't want anyone to see them and hurt them again. He or she wants control over who and what enters or hurts their body and may do so through eating—both controlling what enters by eating the food and by the invisibility cloak that fat creates to the predators of their past. When you see an overweight person, it can be a sign that they are at least subconsciously absolutely terrified of anyone seeing the real them because they were taught to shame themselves to their very core. Being overweight allows this to continue. This is probably true for most addictions: the addiction itself keeps them in the state of shame they are familiar with.

Shame keeps us in a state of perceived powerlessness. With deficient energy in our power center, we are unable to set proper boundaries for ourselves—we are unable to love ourselves. My adult self often doesn't step in and say I've had enough food to eat and push it away. I'm caught in an endless cycle of pleasing and resisting. When boundaries were held in unloving ways, we were not taught the real purpose of them: to love our whole self through our choices and actions. This is why it's also imperative for parents to model loving themselves for their children. We do what we saw, not what we were told. The conflicting message that we received; that we were "bad" people for not cleaning our room or eating junk food creates this treacherous dynamic where we feel shame and resistance when making a choice rather than only viewing it as an opportunity to love and care for our Self. I believe some addictions are just a continued protest to this treatment, a failure to do the work to remember our worth.

Diets don't solve the issue long-term because this belief, and this frightened inner child, can be controlled but will not disappear without healing. The food itself is neutral. It is one with us and cannot and does not want to violate us anymore. Changing our mindset about food means having reverence for it, thanking it, connecting with it, and having the intention that it will fuel us to create with our body, our knowledge, and our voice. Shifting our focus to giving from our mouth rather than taking, through our speaking and connecting with others is paramount. You must change the food in your house to reflect your new intentions. Do not keep food around that you feel violates you. Keep only foods that you feel love from. The intention is to fuel. Release the shame. Do not violate yourself anymore. Love yourself enough to spend ten more minutes chopping fresh fruits and vegetables to add to your meal. You are worthy of the time and attention a vibrant meal takes!

Part of overcoming any addiction is to fully envision the reality we WANT to create, the one that reflects the US we know exists as our essence, and set our intentions at every moment to line up with that vision. If our desired feelings are to be happy, joyful, free to fly - then we can't live with intentions that keep us tethered, feeling shameful, angry, resentful, and bitter. We must spend time daily to see ourselves as we want to be, and feel into that vision. Any activity that takes us away from that high-frequency state of Love must be ceased, or we won't reach our vision. If we are unwilling or unable to do this, then there is some part of us that is still too terrified to step into this vision, too terrified to receive our own love. Or, it means that something or someone about our situation is not lining up with our vision and we are so disappointed about that that we return to the substances which make us forget this is our current situation.

Love Yourself Through It

For all addictions, ending them ultimately means making a choice to have daily, adequate self-care by choosing to love your Self. As my

155

mentor Suzi Lula says, "God has entrusted me with my Self, and I want to care for the precious life that I have been given." Again, self-care is anything that nourishes you in mind, body, or spirit. It is taking care of your physical health; sleeping, eating well, avoiding addictive foods or substances, moving your body, taking baths, wearing clothes or presenting yourself in a way that feels authentic and empowering no matter your size. It's taking care of your mental and emotional health through meditation, connecting with your tribe, coaching or therapy for trauma relief, and journaling. And most importantly, it's having a regular spiritual practice of daily meditation, prayer/energy work, journaling, music—to connect to your higher self and intuition as well as raise your vibration.

Just focusing on what we need to REMOVE from our lives makes sense to our logical brain, but it terrifies our emotional mind. Our emotional brain needs to think about what our desired feelings are in that moment when the choice presents itself: Do we want to feel loved or not? Here is our chance to end the feelings from our childhood—here is the opportunity to live a life feeling boundlessly loved! It doesn't matter to our brain to think about how bad our addiction is for us, or even others, and why. It needs to know how it makes us FEEL right now and how we could FEEL if we stopped it. It needs to picture us there. It needs to see us as WORTHY of getting there.

The loving choice is to take the time to plan, prepare, clean, tidy, maintain, organize, and just check in. The loving option is to take the time we need to make a loving choice for ourselves, every time. It may feel selfish in the beginning but putting ourselves first and doing the things that bring us joy puts us in alignment with our soul and raises our vibration. In other words, self-care/Self-love provides REAL bliss so we won't need to continue to use a substance to search for synthetic bliss through a dopamine hit.

In my home, just putting some structure into the day so that I achieve the things I need to does still give me a dopamine hit when I cross them off my list, but also removes the underlying anxiety in my body that would generally lead me to mindlessly snack. Rather than procrastinate or feel lazy, just getting up and doing a small cleaning task and being present while I do it makes me feel productive and also helps me move my body. I like to set timers for 5-10 minutes and only do a task for that long, that tricks my brain into thinking it's not as daunting as it would normally appear and sets up my reward system to know that as soon as it's done I'm moving on to some other more "desirable" task. Ultimately, though, I had to get to a place where I truly knew what it meant to love myself with every choice and every action. I had to see where I was living in the extremes and seek balance rather than feel guilt or shame for residing there.

The other danger zone for me is when I'm attempting to squeeze more into my day by staying up late to work on projects. What I perceive as a need for food is actually my body desiring for me to go to sleep and get adequate rest. Sleep is so high on the self-care scale because it re-energizes us. If you are running on empty, you cannot make a loving choice and still not give your body what it needs first. You will be tricked into thinking that you can have/do whatever you want because you are pushing past what you need and still running on empty. You're going for the lit match rather than adding logs to the fire.

As the circumstances that caused my stress begin to disappear, there is less need to protect myself from them. As I put myself first and really focus on what I can do for myself each day to put myself in that happy state of being loved by myself, I have less and less need to get my good feels from unhealthy places. But we must have some structure in place to make sure we accomplish this. You need to do some planning every week or every day or whatever works for you so that what you do with your time and what you'll eat is right for you. You decide what tasks will help you to feel better and then schedule them. Following your plan over and over again eventually makes doing the task mindless, and those kinds of habits that we don't have to think about help our brain with its desire to be as efficient as possible. When I'm REALLY struggling with a chore I dislike, I think about how fortunate I am to do it in the first place. *I'm so lucky to pay these bills right now, it means I have the money to pay them. I'm so fortunate that I get to wash these dishes, it means I had food to feed my family. I'm so lucky to clean out my car because I have reliable and safe transportation.* As we do this, we learn to hold our belongings, and us, sacred. We feel their energy and desire to take care of them. We feel OUR energy and know that we will feel better by taking care of everything around us.

So, whether you are the one with the addiction or it's only your spouse, the focus must be on YOU. Being your best self not only makes your life better so that their addiction may not even affect you anymore, but it also helps you inspire them to change as well. Getting enmeshed with their energy (letting their actions control how you feel or believing your actions control how they feel), feeling like you must change them, feeling like you must help them, not being able to see them in pain, giving them ultimatums that launch them into fear, and especially shaming them, all contribute further to the addiction, and that is the opposite of loving them.

Authentic Action Step #8:

Do three <u>loving</u> things for yourself every day this week.

Write them down as you do them.

Chapter 9: *You're Cheating Yourself*

I t's so heartbreaking when the person we have loved a long time cheats. Finding out can be so drama-filled; an anonymous letter detailing what someone thinks you should know, a call from the other woman herself, finding all those late nights at work were spent in a bed on the other side of town...

Of course, we feel betrayed. We feel angry and upset. How could he DO that to us? To our kids? The people that love him most? How could he just walk away from everything?

We are so deep in our own grief that we, of course, don't look at our role at all. She overlooks the fact that she's had nothing but snarky reactions to her husband's behavior. She forgets when she pulled away from his embrace. She ignores when she didn't offer support during his accomplishments. He overlooks when he spent hours with his buddies while we fell asleep alone. He disregards all of the times she tried to connect, but he was too busy looking at his phone. We all overlook our role in the co-creation of cheating because that's what we've always done. The truth is, no outcome is created alone in a relationship.

That is not to blame anyone either. We just have to take a step back—or many flights up—and look down at the situation from above, look at the big picture. What were the thousands of causes and effects that got us to this point where someone is done - and either cheats or leaves? Even if all we can come up with is the fact that we chose and married say, a sex addict, we still participated in the cause. We still chose him or her. Just as we marry the alcoholic that doesn't take care of his body or the food addict that doesn't take care of hers. Unless we were comatose the entire relationship, signs were there. We ignored them.

Lies and Deceit

Because I met my husband directly after the man that tried to talk his way around the fact that he was dating several women, I came into the relationship already owning my trust issues. From the start, I explained to him that I had a hard time trusting and I would not stalk him, but I would appreciate honesty. What I didn't realize was that I had control over the conditions that breed dishonesty. What I've learned is that my reaction to the truth dictates the amount of truth someone will share with me. When I found out my husband spent a lot of money and went into a tirade about it, that was the last time he was honest when he spent a lot of money.

If you tell someone in your circle that your husband lied to you, even if it was a super minor event, they'd likely tell you that it's a deal breaker. The mental noise about the lying then becomes a more significant motivator than the act itself. Instead of looking at the actual behavior, we think we can't trust them now, and what does that mean? Now they're going to do even bigger things behind our back. The relationship is doomed.

Before you jump to that conclusion, however, know that when someone lies to you, it usually means they were too afraid of you to tell you the truth. Think back to when you were a teenager. The more your parents yelled at you, shamed you ("How *could* you??"), or punished you, the more you did behind their back. It's likely that you honed your skills at deception and storytelling as a teenager just trying to live your life!

If, when your husband tells you the truth, you go on the attack, then he will start hiding what he does or lie about it. To foster honest communication, we must be honest and transparent ourselves, and respond rather than react when they're honest with us.

Breaking this dynamic once it's present is a challenge. After we got home from the store tonight, my husband hugged me and said he wanted to go out and was going to fill the gas tank in his car. Oh, how I wish he would learn to fill his own tank, but that's another book. Anyway, he was gone much longer than it would take. I kept probing him when he got home, trying to figure out what he actually did. He lied a bit at first, trying to claim the pump was slow (really, dear?) and finally revealed that he'd stopped to buy something he'd been wanting. I just said, "Okay."

In the past I would have shamed him about spending money—*"Why would you spend money we don't have?!"*—and do you know where that got me? Suffice it to say, it didn't improve his spending habits. I wish I could undo all of the damage I did with my reactions, but all I can do now is re-build the trust I lost and let him know that I am a safe person to tell the truth to, especially when it comes to our money.

The Care and Keeping of a Relationship

Our relationships create their own energy field, just as we each have our own. What we put into that field determines how the relationship will grow. It's just like a plant that needs consistent sun, a little water, and sometimes a dose of fertilizer. It needs warm conditions to grow in. It requires regular attention, we can't just neglect a plant for a week or two and expect it to continue to thrive. Each relationship in our lives—whether it's our spouse, money, our job, kids, etc.—needs DAILY attention. It requires at least a little bit of your time to check in, provide value, give attention, and show them you recognize their worth.

Many of us—probably most of us—neglect our relationships for months or even years at a time. Especially when the kids come, and we are so focused on helping those helpless little seedlings grow, we forget that our relationship with our spouse needs just as much attention. And that isn't to blame one person in the relationship - BOTH need to help it continue to grow. One person cannot save it no matter how great a gardener they are. They are lying to themselves if they think they can do it all on their own. Both of you must tend to the garden daily.

As we continue to grow, we often start moving away from the level of consciousness our spouse is at. Connection is no longer even possible as the two of us are speaking an entirely different language. For a cell phone to work, it has to tune to the right frequency and right channel to begin the transmission. Then the other phone has to do the same and acknowledge the call before you can even start a conversation.

A marriage or relationship is just like that. If we stop tuning in to the same frequency because one grows and the other doesn't, connection is not possible. I've been married eight years now and even getting an acknowledgment when you are the same frequency can be difficult at times! Some days the phone just keeps ringing...

But that doesn't mean someone is at fault for where they are at in their growth. We are each on our own path, on our own journey, and have a whole lifetime (and several previous lifetimes if you understand reincarnation) that put us exactly where we are in this exact moment. This is why signing a contract to declare that you will stay with someone for the entire rest of your life is an absurd undertaking. Yes, perhaps you'll find someone who is at a similar place when you meet and is committed to keep growing while you're together, but everyone hits bumps in the road.

Addictions are easy to abstain from under controls but very hard to actually overcome - often replaced by a different habit. Sometimes life doesn't deliver the karma for each action as quickly as we would like. Sometimes it takes great suffering to awaken, and often it ends in death anyway.

So the idea of someone betraying you is an illusion. No matter how innocent we want to feel, we're both responsible for the current status of our relationship. Nothing is indeed a surprise if you can look at it from the perspective of cause and effect. Just by signing a paper, we're not entitled to someone's undying devotion no matter how we behave. Our relationship should be an equal partnership, where both parties are committed to loving the other and doing everything they can to improve themselves and grow, so they are both coming from a whole place.

From the moment we meet, we become aware of who the person in front of us is. While we may not even realize our own inadequacies we wish to balance with them, we are always aware that something in them fills a void in us. Once we learn how to fill that void on our own, things change. Or, we may or may not learn, but we stop filling the voids in them. Stereotypically, men will ruthlessly get their needs met. They don't linger on in suffering like women tend to do: once someone who used to meet their needs ceases to do so, they may choose to find someone else that will. The catch is, if the other person is no longer meeting their needs but THRIVING and growing and becoming ever more whole with each passing day, the man is more likely to be unable to look anywhere else. In fact, they may start to feel like they are desperately clinging to that person, and will either eventually rise up to meet them or the relationship will end.

At this moment, as I'm writing this, I would not be surprised one bit if my husband came home and said he cheated on me. Between the changes from having kids and my own growth, I'm sure that I'm not

163

meeting a lot of his needs that I used to. The difference is that I'm standing firm in knowing what my needs and boundaries are. I'm inviting him to join me at my new level of consciousness, and he's aware of that and rising to meet me. The other difference is that he is also more aware of authentic versus artificial needs than the "average man." A lot of things men cheat for, like sex, cuddles, ego-stroking, etc. are not deal breakers for him. He has a healthy grasp of artificial versus authentic power.

Outside of the idea of need is just opportunity. My husband has said, "You're only as faithful as your options." I don't doubt this is true. When the intentions behind the act of sex are to feel powerful and excited rather than to have a very intense energy exchange, they may, of course, go for someone who fits that intention if the option is there. Our human nature is to explore sexually, and this is not to give everyone a free pass to do so, but we were wired this way. However, what I didn't even understand until I read *Quantum Love* by Dr. Laura Berman is how amazing sex can be with the same partner just by changing the *intention* behind it each time. It really is a choose-your-own-adventure kind of activity.

Making Waves, Making Love

Before you even get undressed, set the intention for what you want to experience during intimacy. Do you want to exchange love? Do you want to go for the gold and have an hour of mind-blowing sex? Sex to me used to be all about approval, I used to just want to make the other person feel good, so I would be worthy. I was entirely in my head during the encounter, thinking about everything rather than just surrendering to the sensations. The subconscious intention was probably just to be accepted. Now I know that I can set the intention for precisely what I want to feel during or after the intimacy and that changed everything.

Sex is so much more than the friction of genitals. To have intense, mind-blowing sex, you must be able to harness the energy in your body before, during, and after the physical activity. Visualizing energy moving around your body, and between your bodies, and even creating an unending circle of energy with the orgasm after, is far more powerful than any porn-esque hotel rendezvous. This kind of energy exchange is only possible in a very trusting relationship. I mean, think about it for a minute, do you want to visualize this love energy moving through you and into some random guy you just met? Would you feel comfortable doing that? Would you have the loving energy for them? I think most of us don't let our guards down enough to do that right away. And if you aren't ready to make it an exchange of energy, why bother to just have mundane, boring, friction-based sex? How are a few seconds of a bliss state worth whatever you've put on the line for that encounter?

Yet men (typically) do it every day. Bless their hearts, they don't even know better. They don't even know that for both parties to be fully engorged and have these life-altering exchanges, they must be still and focused first. They must know how to visualize the movement of energy. They both must be relaxed and open-hearted. Just five minutes of an energy moving exercise before sex could change your whole night. If your intention is merely to orgasm in whatever fashion that first arrives for you, another person is not even required. The point of two people being intimate is to access another dimension together, to have a full union of the energy of your souls.

We are just energy. We have bodies, but WE are energy. Our soul is energy. And our soul's home is love. Now, for me, sex only of the body is like asleep sex. I want my soul to be involved! I want to have a multi-dimensional experience! Why waste time with anything less? I mean - sometimes - a quickie is just needed to keep the fire going when time is tight - but if you're going to have sex… MAKE LOVE. In the original meaning of that - make the energy of love and connect at the energetic level. Imagine golden energy flowing out of you through your vagina and intertwining with his golden energy which then flows out of him and into you from his heart. Imagine your souls soaring together through the cosmos as one. Being one with the energy within means a state of bliss that lasts well into the next day, or longer.

So, with that said, again, cheating only for sex is such a waste. Especially if you consider the average "other woman" in this case is often someone younger who is far less likely to understand or even be aware of any of this. Perhaps I only speak from my experience, but I feel like for most young women, the image they think men want them to replicate is that of the porn star. It's like WWAPSD (What Would A Porn Star Do)?? I think most of us grow up having NO IDEA what it truly means to make love. Women and men measure themselves by what is being shown in movies or porn—homemade or otherwise—which is always based on the same plot of someone having power over the other. People seeking this kind of encounter are seeking to either have power over or feel powerless to another. They are looking for validation, approval, a false boost to their ego.

See, you can't film the energy exchange I'm talking about. If you did film the kind of lovemaking, it would probably be pretty boring for someone else to watch. Or maybe not… I mean there are whole temples in India covered in statues of sexual positions that are enough to turn some people on. But my point is this: if you're basing your sexual education on porn, you're missing it entirely. If you are attracted to a woman that isn't whole, is looking for your approval, plumping up her bosoms to suit you and allowing you to use and abuse her body, then you have likely never even met a whole woman. Likewise, being attracted to a man that just wants to use you up is creating your own suffering. What would it feel like you to you to be with a man that is whole, kind, and loving? What would it feel like to freely create this mountain of loving energy between you when you're lying naked and vulnerable on the sheets? Allow yourself to imagine it, because that is REAL attraction.

Some people cheat just because they miss having the connection or someone new makes them feel worthy again. Or, you may meet someone and have a very intense energetic connection that you feel you must explore - not necessarily sexually. If you're sure that connection is coming from a state of love and not a state of fear (*ooh, she seems like new wife material*), those types of meetings ARE worth exploring. Perhaps they are a soul you knew in another lifetime. Maybe they arc here to help you on your journey, maybe with your business or your growth. Everyone that you meet, from the person in the drive-through window to the new neighbor down the street, has a purpose in your life. They are here to help you evolve toward wholeness. The ones that you meet and you immediately feel this intense energy between you may have nothing to do with sexual tension and everything to do with some desire you are manifesting. Just recognize the divine in them and be open to whatever is desiring to unfold through you.

When It's Too Late

If your long-term partner has already been "unfaithful," there's no need to yell and scream and cry, though I'm sure at first that is the normal temptation. Remember that they are a person on their own journey. This is a sign that the relationship has long been neglected. What you imagine in your head as existing, didn't exist already. Perhaps it did five years ago, but not lately. We all change every day, sometimes right during the day - one person leaves the house in the morning, and another returns home. That is the point of life: our own evolution toward a loving, fearless state. You aren't guaranteed that your husband won't learn something profound that day and evolve a little more. Do you see how absurd it is that we essentially ask each other to not grow? Would you want someone to go to your child and demand that they sign a paper that says they do declare on this day to cease growth and stay this way for the rest of their lives? Isn't that ludicrous?

But we do so much to make leaving hard. We have kids we're raising that love both of us. We have jobs, homes, cars—every aspect of our life—entwined and entangled together. It's not easy to just leave. I think that's often why people DO cheat, they need the dramatic event to force the dissolution, or want to be sure they have someone else to shack up with so they can continue to pay the bills. Otherwise, we stay comfortable in our discomfort. We relish our way of living with two incomes. Maybe we don't dislike our spouse, we're just leading separate lives under one roof, but no one wants to make the move they know will make someone unhappy, especially if it's their kids.

The interesting thing about leaving a relationship that you are no longer satisfied with is that you will find another relationship that becomes exactly like it, unless you learn the lessons you're meant to learn in this one. The next partner will continue to mirror the parts of you that are not yet healed: The elements of you that don't know how to stand up for yourself, how to identify your needs, how to voice them, how to respond rather than react, how to transform an argument rather than "win" one.

And the chances of you learning these lessons on your own are slim because intellectually understanding something and responding differently when triggered are worlds apart. The only advantage to starting over is that perhaps it's less of a turbulent ride as your new partner should have limited adapting to do.

Infidelity is an illusion. It's not a betrayal but a culmination of a myriad of causes and effects that both parties in a relationship had a role in. From the time we sign a contract to do the impossible, we pretend we possess the other, pretend we own them, pretend they owe us anything, and pretend we'll never change. We can't pretend anymore. Seek out a spiritual partnership when you're whole or transform what you have through your own evolution.

Whether you stay with a partner that has cheated is a choice only you can make, and it will probably feel like it has been made for you. Either you will find yourself sharing a bed once again, or you will find all of your belongings in a new space. Life will move you exactly where you need to go, and if you can't decide what to do, it means you're not ready to make a choice because none of your options are right for you... yet.

The biggest obstacle is to repair trust, which means that you must take a long, hard look to see if you even trust yourself to do what's right for you; what's in alignment with your essence, what feels authentic at your core.

You weren't cheated on because you aren't worthy, you were cheated on because you stopped treating yourself as worthy. They found what THEY (in their current state of consciousness) needed elsewhere, now it's time for you to find what YOU need.

Remember your own divinity and every circumstance in your life will rise up to reflect it. If you want a better reflection from your relationships, change who's looking in the mirror.

Authentic Action Step #9:

Accept that your spouse has already cheated, whether they have or not. Accepting that you've already "lost" them means you never have anything to lose, which will loosen your grip.

Embrace a deep knowing that you will be okay no matter what happens.

Chapter 10: *Irreconcilable Differences*

I think the majority of marriages get to a place where we aren't repulsed by our spouse, aren't scared of them, aren't being abused by them, but we are so disconnected that we get stuck in a loop of analyzing the situation. We get stuck trying to decide whether or not they are a big enough jerk to disrupt our entire lives, so we can leave them and get as far away as possible.

We are often just one big argument away from Google-ing the nearest divorce lawyer and launching our family into complete chaos.

Divorce

The word "divorce" means to dissolve one's marriage, and "dissolve" in this sense means to "annul or put an end to." So, when we divorce someone, it means we put an end to our experience of growing with them. If we have children, however, it means that we continue our experiencing of growing with them, but in separate homes, as you remain committed to the new version of that relationship at least until the children turn 18. Even then the former spouse will still be in your life in some form as a loved one of your children—or an unloved one. Either way, part of your energy is likely to remain attached. They may continue to be involved in grandchildren's birthday parties, your child's special events, etc.

As long as you have children with someone, you can never truly write them out of your story. While the form of the marriage no longer exists, the relationship remains. And, often, because most relationships are the play of two inner children, that relationship becomes intensely strained and destructive. I think it is extremely rare to find two divorced, whole co-parents. Usually, the inner child REALLY comes out when it's time to go to court and discuss all of the reasons why the relationship is over and who should get what. The feeling of rejection is a reliable time machine back to our hurting, tantrumming inner child parts.

You will deal with a family court that has little knowledge of your child's developmental needs. Even if you have an exclusively breastfed infant, you'll likely have to split your time with the co-parent. Hopefully, they are lovingly attuned to your child, but if either of you is in and out of deep fear, resentment, or anger—the child is ultimately who suffers for it.

My parents separated when I was eight years old. We had been in Michigan, visiting my grandparents, and returned home to find them sleeping in separate rooms. I remember there was intense discussion and then someone finally said they were going to no longer live together. It seems like quite quickly my dad moved out into some rental home and before I knew it, we were trick-or-treating around an unfamiliar neighborhood.

At first, I didn't quite grasp or understand it, but then the pain started to flow through the house in tears and words. The bickering began. My biggest memory from my parents' divorce was the phone calls. I don't even know what they were about, but my mom and dad would be on the phone and then suddenly she would yell and hang up. It felt like it happened every other day. Then he would call back and get hung up on again. I was always confused, because my mom seemed to be much happier without my dad and had a long list of cons, but also seemed very bitter and rejected at the same time. Life was tense. We couldn't even talk about him at home without the conversation going south. Loving him seemed to be a betrayal, and I tried to take on the burden of "making" her happy.

One Christmas, probably early in this process, our dad was invited. I was told over and over that they weren't getting back together, this was just for today, and I didn't understand why they kept telling me this. In retrospect, the divorce itself really didn't bother me that much, it was the emotional toll of a parent suffering that got to me. The (what felt like) constant bashing of or inquiry about the other parent (which alternated depending on whomever I was with) confused me. How do I show up for both parents? Loving them both equally seemed to be out of the question all of a sudden. It felt disloyal. Space for my own feelings and needs seemed to be non-existent.

I feel like we visited a counselor once or twice and went to something I imagine was a child of divorce support group at a large building with other kids, but the most I remember about that was making a train out of candy. I remember being told repeatedly that it wasn't my fault, but I had no idea why they would think I would even think it was my fault, until they repeated it so much that I wondered if it actually was my fault. I would later find out that most of their fights did center around the way we were being raised, and primarily how much money was being spent on us. It seemed so disingenuous to me to go talk to a stranger about the divorce and my feelings about it instead of my own parents, who mostly acted less mature than we did about the whole situation. My parents were almost entirely unable to hold any space for our feelings, but this was nothing new. I'm not sure if they ever went to any individual counseling after the decision to separate, and as a coach now, I feel speaking to someone weekly is imperative for anyone going through such a traumatic event. From what I've read and experienced, however, it's critical to talk to the RIGHT person. There's a good chance that therapists in the 80's, when they separated, actually steered their clients toward divorce, buying into the idea that our happiness is controlled by external factors.

Now I don't even remember if details were shared with us directly or if we just overheard conversations with other adults, but I learned more about my parents than I ever should have known. I learned more about the process of the divorce than I wanted to.

That case dragged on two years. Finances became extremely tight, and fear over them loomed. The mindset about money had always been one of lack (and was one of the primary drivers for the divorce), but now it became even worse.

Then, my grandmother started to live with us part of the year, and finally all of the time, before we moved twelve hours north into her home and left behind everything I loved; my woods, my pool, my house, my friends, and my father.

Up in Michigan and entering my teen years, things were especially dismal, and I was very sad and depressed. Eventually, my father also moved to Michigan (both parents were from there) with his new wife and going back and forth was extremely stressful. The guilt when I got home about missing my dad, even though my mom was so busy with work and trying to survive that we rarely connected, manifested physically as severe stomach aches and feeling sick and miserable most of the time. While she used her nursing skills to treat the symptoms, she unconsciously contributed to the cause of the pain, so hurt that I'd be sad to be back home with her after a weekend away. I was sick and weighed down by the guilt I thought I had to carry. My heart was in two places.

I feel like people often act as though the child will just adapt, they'll be fine, that it's the spouse who has to recover. I remember being told to "get over it," "move on," "shit happens." It seems like divorce is viewed just like changing schools or moving—they'll adjust. This couldn't be further from the truth. The child is going through a divorce, too. They are experiencing the worst breakup of all, second only to the death of a loved one. This trauma causes the heart to eventually shut down from the pain. The hurt for a child who had no say in this breakup is tremendous. Even if they still see both parents regularly, the relationship is forever changed by both the new circumstances and the damage to each parent in the process—the pain-body they now carry—meaning they have often have an entirely new parent. One who is also in so much pain that they rarely are fully present with the child, and often incapable of providing the empathy and support their child needs. Imagine being in agony yourself and trying to adapt to your new life, while holding space for the pain of two or three children who are already much more in their emotional brain than the adult.

Visiting my dad was no walk in the park either; he could be very controlling and at times just uncomfortable to be around. With a new wife, it felt like we were just a weekend accessory rather than a wanted relationship. It wasn't long before my brother stopped visiting him and it felt like I was in the middle of a war, bouncing between both sides. I felt very much like a traitor at one house and guilt for that at the other.

Nothing about my years 9-17 was joyful. It wasn't the divorce that caused suffering, it was the choices made after that separation that did. It was the emotional tug of war my parents unconsciously played with my heart. Little did I know then how empathic I am and how their own energy from their suffering was being absorbed daily by me. I know that at times they must have felt the environment before the divorce was less healthy for us, and perhaps I would have been more aware of that as we got older, but all I remember from those first eight years is the good.

So now, eight years into my own marriage and two kids later, every time divorce enters my mind as an option, I relive everything I experienced as a child. The seeming magical first eight years of my life versus the emotional misery of the remainder of my childhood. I've spent so much of my adulthood stuck at age eight or less. What would my own kids experience? Besides the dramatic changes in their lifestyle due to finances, what would the emotional toll be?

Yet, what is the emotional toll of living in a house with two already disconnected parents? What best serves them? If they must leave to be able to soar, then they must go. If they must leave to be safe, then the choice is already made.

When the divorce causes one or more parents to become less, rather than more, whole, the child will ultimately suffer greatly. A child that has at least one parent that they are attached to and can depend on is far more resilient than a child that has a "perfect" home and life but unreliable parents.

I didn't have fantastic connections with either parent to begin with, and what I did have became incredibly strained after the divorce, but that's ultimately not what completely rocked my world. Children thrive on structure and routine. There is no age where our belongings define us more than childhood. We feel that we know who we are based on what we have, what we are attached to. It wasn't until we had to leave our home, our friends, and our state, and that structure crumbled around me, that the divorce truly bothered me. Looking back, I can see how nurtured I was my entire childhood by the experiences I had in the nature surrounding our home, and with the animals we kept as pets inside it. The house itself was friendly to me, feeling like my caretaker, even like a mother. When I recall it now, it has a mother energy. I spent most of my time playing alone inside or outside, enjoying the freedom we had as homeschoolers without demands on our time. Our summers were filled with fresh watermelon and pool adventures. I climbed trees and laid in the sunshine, the aroma of the bark and chatter of the birds lulling me to sleep. South Carolina was a beautiful state, with the mountains in the distance and blue skies following me everywhere.

It was my grandma moving in that started to crack everything. Then the transition from unstructured homeschooling to a public school I felt lost in. And finally, the move from my sunny Carolina home to the bitter cold and gray skies of the north. The first year in Michigan it snowed on my birthday and, while novel, it was depressing. All of these changes were motivated by the fear of security. It wasn't the divorce that finally broke my heart totally into pieces, it was a hurting parent's choice to move that ultimately did.

Meanwhile, my dad seemed to be perfectly content with our minimal weekend visits. I missed him, but by that point I was also afraid to miss him, and all of the stories I overheard about how awful he was started to wear on me. The timing of our move north was no accident, as it was at the exact same time that my father remarried and moved his new wife (who was an old flame) to our town. I imagine that was just too much for my mom and she left.

While my dad was already rarely mentally present with us (he's very much a planner and a do-er), being at his home without any of my things or my mother just felt like some strange trip I was on. I felt like an inconvenience to him and was not a part of planning any of the many things he came up with for us to do. I very much felt like I had to fit into his story, I wasn't an integral part of the creation of it.

It is hard to witness the inner child of both of your parents at play, but it is even harder to live with the choices those inner children make. The child longs for the adult self of each parent to come forth.

When Divorce is an Option

During the hardest season of our marriage, I wasn't silent about my anger and resentment at all. Pretty much anything he did would get some flippant comment from me about divorce or leaving. It wasn't necessarily a threat as just my real thoughts and feelings about what was going on. I was learning to use my voice, and I probably told him every day that I was ready to leave if nothing changed.

Whether he believed me or not is a different story. I had repeatedly said from the time we met that I would never divorce once we had kids. I had been through hell when my parents separated, and I would never do that to them. When this started, I did as much research as I could about what was best for my children. A good friend shared how her parents fought all of the time and she just always wished they would get a divorce. I heard other children of divorced parents say how it was the best thing that happened to them. Yet professionals advised that it was important to maintain the same home for them as long as possible, which matched my experience.

What began to become clear to me as the massive difference in the child's perception, is that divorcing so you can become whole is one thing, but divorcing and never becoming whole is entirely different. Divorcing so you can finally allow your true self to unfold is means a glorious future. The heavy learning is done. Divorcing when you have yet to even uncover the wounds and emotional healing you have left to do is just a traumatic way to continue to learn through fear and doubt. The patterns repeat. The exact same dynamic that you have now will repeat in the next relationship. It may even happen in your relationship with the child that is more likely to inherit your ex's characteristics. The divorce will probably be bitter and create even deeper wounds.

Yet our situation was mild compared to what most children go through. They didn't have a custody battle, and we were never forced to see him. They never returned to court after the divorce was finalized, as far as I know, and even when I stopped talking to him years later, he never demanded we see him or accuse my mom of turning us against him or "parental alienation."

My parents were terribly different people when it comes down to it. Not only did they swing between the narcissist/empath patterns, but they also grew up so differently that the day-to-day tasks of living and raising a family had stark contrasts to their individual beliefs and desires. My mom ended up wanting to homeschool us and worked as a nurse alternate shifts so that we were with her during the day and my dad when she wasn't home. They became ships in the night, rarely getting to spend much time together, as she would work weekends as well. My dad wanted to be together and wanted her to put us in school so they could work the same shift and make that happen. We were the most important thing in my mom's life, and she would have moved mountains to give us the best she could. She just wanted us to experience better than she had growing up. My parents had extremely different views on money, and anytime she spent money on us it was a big fight. I could go on and on about household tasks, pets, décor, clothing, toys, etc.

I believe toward the end, my mom likely felt unappreciated and resentful, and my dad probably felt neglected and empty.

And this exactly described my own marriage.

Who Wants the Divorce?

If you are in a position where the possibility of divorce looms as a valid or even desirable option, I invite you to see who wants the divorce. Is it the adult self, who can no longer tolerate the antics of their spouse's inner child? Or is it your own inner child, begging for its needs to be met? If it is the latter, divorce will not bring you the peace you desire for very long. As I said, if you already have children, the torment will continue as you navigate co-parenting. If not, you will continue to see your patterns play out in subsequent relationships (even friendships) until such time that your adult self is able to step up and heal; until you take another step toward wholeness.

If you don't have children, this may be a good option. You may wish to pull all of your energy back and go play with someone else to learn your lessons. Maybe you like variety. But the reality is that the experiences that are needed for your growth will continue to occur until you recognize them and learn the lessons. The best question to ask is, "How is this serving me? What is this here to teach me?"

If you do have children and have already done a lot of evolving and your spouse hasn't kept up, the question now is, do you wait to see if they will? What is your level of commitment? What have you already tried? Often, a new way of communication can start to turn things around. Where you may have just decided to stay zen and keep your mouth shut, speaking your truth and conveying your needs is necessary. Will you be the one to help your spouse evolve? Not necessarily. As you change patterns and respond differently when conflict arises, something may click that urges them to grow. But there is an equal chance that they may not be ready or willing to do this growth. For some, the process of awakening only happens when the current conditions are unbearable. A lot of big and necessary changes in life are pushed by this.

When fear arises, welcome it as a loving messenger. It's a very loud friend that has entered your body to get you to act. Act is not the same as panic and freak out. Act means that you accept what is and now you take action to find a solution. Taking action in a relationship often means having a productive conversation. Most of us get caught up in our focus on the problem itself, which helps no one. We torment ourselves recalling all of the steps that got us here. The ego will step in with a bunch of "How dare they? How could she? Why did I do that? How could I have been so stupid?!" Ultimately, that is futile. That may stoke some kind of fire, but a destructive fire is not what you need unless burning the relationship down IS the only choice.

What You Focus on Grows

There have been many times in recent years that I've considered divorce and I never, ever, ever, in a million years thought I would have. I remember now the very first time I felt like I'd made a grave mistake marrying him. It was when my daughter was very little, and I can't remember the exact scenario but I was trying to take a shower, and it just hit me: what have I done? I believe that at that moment my intention changed and my level of commitment changed. The reality is that our thoughts create our reality, and thus my thoughts delivered. My new view of my husband meant I continued to find evidence of these new beliefs about him everywhere. I was no longer looking for the good or delighting in his quirks. Nearly everything he did was proof that I wasn't in a relationship that was serving me. What you believe about your partner is what you will see. I promise you this is true. If you don't believe me, look at every new relationship ever. When twenty observers know that it's doomed, the two people in it will always think the other hung the moon. If you start believing this about your spouse every day, watch what happens.

Likewise, believing that they are a selfish beast who is wasting your remaining years of youth and vitality, will make it so.

There are many, many ways to attempt to reboot a marriage once you're in a shitty place. Divorce is to a long-term marriage what spanking is to parenting: It is often the mindless reaction, the lazy choice, the attempt to punish the other rather than love ourselves. It can be looking personal growth in the face and running the other way. No one outside of you is going to make you any happier than you presently are. This is an inside job.

The question is: Do you have room to grow and stay in a high vibration place in your present relationship? Do you dedicate time to nurturing the relationship, and are you able to receive their love? Are you able to remain in a state of love even when they are brutal? Do you enter their suffering or merely allow it? Do you have confidence in your ability to set boundaries? What is for your highest growth? What is for their highest growth? If separating is the only thing that will allow growth, then that is the answer, but it will be delivered without a doubt and not through strenuous analyzing and decision making. Otherwise, the entire purpose of relationships is for growth and only when that turns to stagnancy on either end do you need to shift, change, or transform something about your present experience.

Thank and Release

This is your present reality. Tell the ego that you have this. Love the scared parts of you and let them know you realize there's a lesson here. Accept. Speak to your higher self, God, Source, the universe. I had to sit down with the lessons my husband had taught me and thank the universe for them. I had to view our relationship as a karmic role that was necessary for my evolution. I kid you not, the day I energetically thanked my higher self for the lessons and released it all, he came home a different person. Mind you, he was not physically involved in that process at all. It was like a meeting with the universe, here, in my office. I sat in my chair, closed my eyes, and imagined connecting to both of our higher selves, our souls. I spoke out loud and said that I can see the big picture now. I can see what he is here to teach me. I see the lesson, and I'm grateful for it. Then I energetically sent love to him for the experience and his role in my growth.

Ask your intuition for assistance in how to move forward. Call a coach to help you release the emotions and gain clarity. You may do some energy healing with tapping, Reiki, EMDR, or somatic experiencing. But ultimately, the answer is not outside of you—you always have all of the answers you need within. How to move forward will come to you once you fully surrender to what is. Ending the relationship is ultimately not a choice to make with your mind. The "choice" will be made for you – you may wake up one day and feel your body move you out, or your spouse may be the one to leave. It will be as mentally effortless as brushing your teeth. Thinking about leaving is your mind living in the future, which doesn't exist anywhere but your mind. Leaving can be a portal to new growth but so can staying. Only those that are willing to make the leap will be moved to leave their current situation. They will not go until they are ready for the jump, rather than afraid of where they're jumping from.

As I've shared, when men are upset or triggered, they tend to default to anger. Women tend to internalize and go to guilt or shame. These are low-frequency energies, and nothing is created or nurtured there. Catch yourself in this place and make the conscious choice to shift up, to turn the dial. Whatever is going to happen, it's for you, and you are fully equipped to handle it.

Communication

Sometimes we need to visualize ourselves at the top of a mountain, looking down at the situation from a higher perspective. What can we change? What are our priorities? Take out a notepad and write your priorities on it, the things that are absolutely the most important to you. You might write; "Our health, the quality of our children's experiences, connecting with our children..." Sit down with your spouse and compare lists. With each priority, list what you feel about it and why you need it. Allow your spouse to do the same with their list. This isn't defending anything, this is to help you understand where you both are and why something is important. Once you know why, you can then help to meet those needs with your partner. This knowledge will also guide your choices, especially around the kinds of jobs you work or how you spend your money. When I realized "our health" was at the top of my list, it blew me away since that it was one of the last things I spent money on!

What if your spouse won't even sit down for a talk like that? Then clearly you already have a severe breakdown in communication that you must attempt to transform. Do your talks usually involve shame or personal attacks? My best advice for a good discussion with a spouse is to get in the car with them and go somewhere far away. For some reason, people that are usually super closed and shutdown will open right up during a car ride. I think 99% of the major discussions we've had in our marriage have taken place on either a motorcycle or in a car traveling down the road. For my husband, I know it's helpful to him to have no distractions that he can escape in. He's also kinesthetic and moving while talking helps him process. Otherwise, when approaching anyone for a serious conversation, ask them if it's a good time to talk, or let them know that you want to have a talk at a specific time.

The key is to getting a man to help is to invite them in by expressing what you're sensing or observing and allow them to come to the solution, rather then directly telling them what to do. *"Brian doesn't have any shoes on." "Sarah hasn't eaten lunch, she's got to be really hungry." "I won't be done with this project for another hour and the kids get out of school in a bit."* Give them a chance to let the wheels turn.

The key to productive conflict resolution is to first recognize and validate the feelings and needs in the other and then state your own feelings and needs, but with factual statements that don't include "when you.."—this is about what YOU need, not what they do. You may find that just validating their feelings and needs allows them to open up. Let them talk. Be as silent as possible; imagine you are merely witnessing what they are saying, even if they're talking about you. There's no need to fix them or change their mind. Reflect back the major points of what they've said lovingly, with a friendly tone, to be sure you understand and they feel heard. Allow them to talk some more. Let them get it all out like they are popping bubble wrap and need to get every last satisfying bubble. Once you feel like it's all out, and they seem complete, they may naturally move on to seeing things a different way, or start talking about you. If not, share your feelings and needs with "I" statements: "When both kids need me, and I'm trying to get food on the table or clean, I feel overwhelmed and angry. I need help balancing the care of our house with the care of our children." Then you can ask if they have any ideas for solutions, or you can make a specific, actionable request, like, "Would you be willing to engage and play with the kids for 30 minutes so that I can cook?" or, "Would you be willing to cook so that I can attend to the kids?"

It is not enough to just state your complaint without making a request. They cannot read your mind. They may not realize that you are even asking them for help, it may seem like you are just venting. Be ready to involve them in finding the solution or have that specific request for them—as long as it's something reasonable. For instance, you can't say "It triggers me when you use that word." As long as their action isn't unconscious and doesn't affect anyone's health or well-being, it's up to you to get to the root of your own triggers. They should not feel like they have to walk on eggshells to make you happy. This request should be something that you genuinely need from them in order to meet your own needs.

Now, if the behavior is unconscious and you are disgusted by it, you can let them know that you will no longer be present for that behavior. So you're letting the person know why you feel that way, what you need, and that you will be moving away from the unconscious behavior. If it continues, that may mean that you go beyond just leaving the room—you may choose to leave the relationship entirely. An example of this is if you have a racist spouse. That behavior is unacceptable and unconscious. You do not have to sit with it, be present to it, or feel the pain of the collective consciousness when it's uttered. Yet you do not have to shame or belittle them when letting them know this no longer acceptable to you. It is what it is. It is up to them to grow. You cannot force them to learn, but you can inspire their growth with your own empathy for whatever pain has led to their perception. Everyone is doing their best, based on their individual conditioning and experiences. If you can get to the root of WHY they're racist, perhaps you can uncover some part of them that is seeking to evolve.

Until you've gotten to this very basic level of adult communication, in most cases, divorce shouldn't be on the table. This is relationship 101 and will serve you in every connection in your life. Go ahead and use your spouse to practice it with. If you can at least a month's worth of adult conversation and decide he's still an incurable jerk, then you probably will know exactly what action to take.

The shedding of the ego happens through willing or unwilling detachment from everything one identifies with. When we are born, we begin to develop this sense of who we are that has nothing to do with who we are. We believe we are our name, our possessions, our roles, our titles, our experiences, our knowledge, our opinions, our house, our job, etc. If we go on the spiritual path, we begin to de-identify with all of these things that have nothing to do with who we truly are. For others, those things start to dissolve. Maybe you lose everything in a fire. Perhaps you're laid off from a job that you love. Something will come along and force you to realize that you still exist without the thing - or the belief - or the title. This process of detaching can be a bit scary, you can feel a bit ungrounded as you tune to a new station and realize there's a whole group of people you're leaving behind at the old one.

Detaching from the role of "husband" or "wife" is imperative for personal growth. There should be no expectation on another just because you are in a marriage, outside of the expectation that you will both to continue to grow and love yourselves. The end goal is not happiness, which comes from within, but wholeness. *I want to live with you because you are fun and I enjoy loving you and being loved by you. I think you will support me in my vulnerability and help me uncover what I have left to heal and transform to become whole.*

Bringing our long-held, fossilized beliefs into the light of consciousness through communication is the first step to transformation and entering a state of wholeness. This is how we heal and release our inner child and fully step into our adult self. The adult self desires to understand those that it's in a relationship with as well as understand where we have room for our own improvement. Every discussion in my life since this journey began is always followed by introspection about what I have left to learn. I've made mistakes, and I continue to learn how to be a better communicator, but approaching conflict with curiosity is the key to resolution. The biggest hurdle for me has been merely voicing more of what I'm thinking. I have been so afraid to share my truth that people I love or people I work with often don't even know who I am, which in turn surprises me and makes me feel unseen and unheard when the truth is I gave them nothing to hear. As an empath, we were shown to be humble, be quiet, be of service. That contributes only to our own demise. When you reserve your vulnerable thoughts just for your husband or journal, the world misses out on the wisdom that your light, your voice, is able to reveal.

Conflict/Communication

So in conflict, first enter the pause. Even if it feels like you are being attacked, raise your vibrational state to that of Love. If anyone is already in the stress response, there is no point in stating your needs or attempting any rational discussion. If that is the case, ask for a timeout, even acknowledge that your wounded inner child has been activated. It is before this escalation that discussion was essential. Take the time you need to allow the emotion to pass, without judging it. When you feel grounded and centered again, you can communicate productively.

No discussion in conflict will be successful without first expressing empathy. When you're able to do this, revisit the issue and lead with empathy, which means putting yourselves in their shoes and reflecting their experience back to them. Only then will they be able to even hear your experience, your needs, and your feelings.

The basic way to approach a productive conversation is this: "I see you are feeling _____, and you need _____. I'm feeling _____, and I need _____. Would you be willing to _____?" Or,

"Do you have any ideas what we could do to achieve this?" Have a specific action for them to take—do not be broad here—and do not stop at only what you are feeling and needing. They should be able to absolutely decide whether they can do that or not on the spot, or start offering solutions.

Offering Empathy

Instead of my own perception when my husband shares, he just needs empathy. He needs me to say: *I see you are in a storm right now.* I have no role in the situation. I don't need to spell it out for him or take it away from him, though that's what I've always done and he's still adjusting. I merely need to let him know that I feel how frustrated he is, without accepting ownership for it or carrying the burden for him.

To be able to look at your husband with empathy, you'll have to drop any and all of judgments of him. And this means that you'll also have to drop all judgments of yourself. This is no easy task. We seem to be hardwired to judge everything around us, labeling it as "good" or "bad." Our brains do this to quickly size things up, so we feel in control. If something makes us unhappy, the ego says it's bad and props us up by giving us a bunch of reasons why we're better, and they're wrong, or the situation shouldn't exist.

Any time we feel under "attack," instead of letting us sit in any pain, our ego chimes in and is like "How dare they! The nerve, after they did all that other shit to begin with! Send them a nasty reply!" We can't even look at the situation objectively because we are so busy avoiding the truth of what is happening: we are triggered, or overreacting to a stimulus. A subconscious belief from our childhood or conditioning is present, and we are adding to the layers and layers it has been buried under by stuffing the emotional pain down once again. It's imperative that we turn off this chatter using meditation.

Empathy means you let them know it's understandable that they feel that way. You may repeat some of what they say, or, in the case of someone who is very out of touch with their feelings, state how you imagine the situation makes them feel. That's all they actually want and need, just like our children. Once they feel that those feelings have been heard and validated, then they can move on. This is so, so hard to do with another adult! Especially one that you have a history of resentment and anger with. The knee-jerk reaction is certainly not to hold the space for them to get this out of their system like we (hopefully) do for a child, especially if they're talking about us. We think they should be able to figure this out on their own by now! We just want the yelling or drama to stop. The sad truth is that most of us weren't raised in emotionally intelligent households. We never learned how to sit with our own pain or change from reaction to acceptance.

Even with empathy, sometimes you will move away from it because the behavior they are using to express their pain is unacceptable. In the case of abuse, empathy may get you to safety in the moment, and then you'll realize you need to leave the situation. Outside of that level of toxicity, you'll get up and leave the room, leave the house, or go back to reading your book. One night I read for forty minutes while he talked and talked and got it all out because nothing I said seemed to help him feel heard. You can energetically send your love and understanding as well, but feel free to carry on with your life if they seem to want to stay stuck in their pain. For the empath that feels the emotional energy of everyone around them, work on having good energetic boundaries and imagining yourself in a glass jar or bubble. Set the intention that you will not take on their energy and they may not use your energy to heal.

Once I realized that I had nothing to fear (in my case he is all bark and no bite) and no role in creating the tantrum, I was able to detach from the situation and see it objectively. Then I was willing to let the man I love sit with his pain and refuse to carry it for him. In this state, you'll notice that you are also able to see if you do bear any responsibility—meaning you'll see if there was a way you could have worked together better or communicated more effectively. Ideally, this is worked out in conversation, but I often find I'm better at deconstructing these on my own if the other person doesn't specifically ask me to show up differently.

This past week I had an issue with a family member, where I'd asked to come for a visit last minute and then, when I wasn't able to go, received a negative response. As I went to offer them empathy, I could see how some of my choices could have been better. I had some communication and structure issues I could improve. It is healthy and normal to look at any role in the co-creation of the event you may have had, but it is not normal to take ownership of another's feelings.

Empathy really is the magic in the moment. Master giving empathy and you'll set the example for how others should treat you when you're upset as well. And you'll do amazing things for your children as they learn how to sit with their feelings and manage their reactions.

To sum it all up:

1. Love is an energetic state you create on your own, by ensuring your needs are met/your energy is re-fueled through self-care, including dropping any energy-consuming thoughts or activities that you can release

2. Arguments are really our inner children screaming for our needs (past or present) to be met, filtered through our ego

3. Good communication of your feelings, needs, and reasonable requests to help you achieve them is vital to a healthy relationship

4. Communication is impossible without leading with empathy

Authentic Action Step #10:

Spend some time identifying the real lesson your partner has been in your life to teach you. Once you understand it, sit quietly, close your eyes, and energetically thank them. Be genuinely grateful. Inform the Universe that you are ready to release the lesson.

Chapter 11: *There is No Fear in Happiness*

If you are unhappy right now, you may have a whole list of reasons why. You may still be seeking things that will make you happy. This is a trick of the ego, the sense of self we have that thinks we need "more" to be satisfied.

Happiness is a place within you. It is a state you are fully capable of and empowered to find all on your own, no matter what your external circumstances are. I used to think I would only be happy if I moved back to the south, out of these frigid winters. I was sure that long-distance move and losing weight was all I needed to finally be happy.

Now I'm able to find happiness every day because I can look beneath the circumstances to deconstruct WHY they're making me unhappy. Once I uncover the why, I can heal it, which means I can accept what the current reality is, and I can move back into a state of love. I realized that I wanted to be in the sunny south again because I felt that state of bliss with the sun on my face, floating in our pool. I can achieve that same bliss in meditation, and I can accept that all living things go through cycles of life and death so they can return to life again. I can honor the Ohio winter now as part of the nature of life itself, rather than fight and resist it. For the southern hemisphere to enjoy summer, I have to experience winter. Do I still love to go find warmth in the winter? Of course! Would I still like to move south? Absolutely! And I will, someday.

But for now, I can't change it and living in Resistanceville is an incredibly unhappy place to call home.

Speaking of moving, have you ever picked up on your ability to feel the energetic frequency of where you live or visit? We can sense when a location has a higher number of people in a higher state of consciousness, a state of or closer to love. In *A New Earth*, Eckhart Tolle writes how he was only able to be in the space to write that book when he was staying on the west coast of North America. The energy of where you live can motivate you to move or take a vacation. As one evolves, they may feel that the energy of their town no longer serves them. When it feels like you must leave and you can, leave. When you can't, accept. Elevate your own frequency. Raise your vibration. Keep your home a space of love by at least staying in a state of acceptance, if not joy.

Feeling like our happiness is dependent on an external condition does keep us stuck. Knowing that you have the power within you, right now, to shift your energy means no more waiting.

Identify the thoughts that are beneath these unhappy emotions and make a conscious choice to change them or release them. Just thinking *I'm unhappy because I live in Ohio and I SHOULD live somewhere else* kept me in a negative state. Changing the thought to *I'm happy no matter where I live* changed my energy.

Once you find the "should" thought, set it on fire and burn it. Stop should-ing yourself now. There is nothing you, or anyone else, SHOULD do. Your present reality is what it is because it's EXACTLY what you needed for your own growth.

You have a husband or wife that is who they are, "faults" and all, because that's EXACTLY what you needed for you to be able to grow and evolve.

You didn't get a college degree and instead took the "harder" path through life because that's EXACTLY what you needed to get to where you are now.

You had a special needs child or a "difficult" child because they are EXACTLY who you needed to shed light on the unhealed parts of you.

There is nothing in this life that exists outside of you. It is all here, perfectly designed for your evolution. Once you are able to know and embrace that fact, you can release the lessons and accept the present.

Life is a series of challenges, my friend. It is not a controlled environment. It is designed to be hard, to be challenging, over and over and over again. Knowing that it's all here for you will allow you to end your own suffering, elevate to a state of happiness independent of your current circumstances, and find freedom in the fact that you are part of a great school that only leads you to your own highest version of you.

Looking for Evidence to Leave/Co-Creation

We have a mental pros and cons list about our husband, and we don't even realize that our day-to-day has devolved into looking for evidence that supports leaving them. Their con list seems to grow exponentially over time, each foul move a red checkmark in their existence in our lives.

What we fail to account for on our list, though we have a vague idea of it, is our own personal contribution to THEIR cons list. When did we give a snarky reply? When did we reject a hug? When did we unconsciously shame them? When did we not even acknowledge their arrival or kiss them goodbye?

Feel Evidence of Love

If you set the intention to have your spouse FEEL evidence of your love today, you inform the field of energy that connects everything that this is your desire. You make it so. You can't think your way to a good marriage. A good marriage must be felt. Moment by moment, you must maintain the intention to feel a high-frequency state of love and collect evidence of the love they have for you and for them to be able to gather evidence of the love you have for them. This will guide your choices and your responses with compassion rather than comparison, and love will be yours for the taking. This is the case between any two people, of any age. When you return to a union between two souls rather than allowing four of you—two hearts + two brains—to run the show, you return to an experience that elevates all involved.

Mirror of the Fear

But what if I'm evolved? I've set the intention? I'm loving? Yet they are constantly in fear? Not over the relationship necessarily, but they seem to walk through life in fear, judging others as a threat, being obsessed with protecting or providing for the family.

They are a mirror, my dear. Something in you is still fearful. Likely, some event happened between you that caused you to start looking for the bad in your partner, and now your existence with them within the context of your relationship is one of fear - always fearful that they are no longer enough. Fear of the divorce. Fear of the decision. Fear of the argument. Fear of how they treat your children. Fear of financial ruin. There is still fear there that you have failed to acknowledge and have wholly denied exists.

Once you drop this relationship-level fear and begin to shift your actions toward your loving intention, then their form-based fear will start to diminish or even disappear as well.

All relationships are a mirror in this way. Sometimes the mirror isn't there to have you heal or set better boundaries or be more authentic, it's there to help you remove fear you can't even see exists. It is asking you to fully wake up to the present moment in a way that you have so far refused to do. Intellectually you think you have; you feel that you have evolved and healed, but the reality is that you have only healed certain aspects of yourself. Other elements remain frightened. Fear of having a bad marriage or a "bad" spouse is still fear.

Renewing your view of the relationship through only the eyes of love will then become a mirror of that love. The fear-based places in your spouse, if you can continue to connect, will dissolve. Do you understand this? Even though you both have fear about entirely different things, it still exists and grows within your relationship's energy field. They are matching your energy.

Once security returns to the relationship, then each soul in it loses a bit of this fear energy each day. It could even happen in one swift moment.

When two souls come together in a relationship, it is by design, I believe it is by karmic agreements created before you were ever born. The body may change, but the person you're with will always push you to your soul's desire of living a fearless life. Each lifetime that we return, we continue to work towards this place. The soul you choose to live most of your life with, and especially to procreate with, is here not only for this push toward growth but for support during the process. They are the biggest fan in your life, and that is why both of you hang on without understanding why sometimes. They, at this soul level, know that they are with you to lift you up to the top, to see you rise to your full authenticity. You know this. Your soul knows that you maintain this connection with them for this purpose. You are aware and were aware when you chose them that they were going to be the soul in physical form that would hold your hand as you walk the earth and make certain that you wouldn't die alone each day, as we all die each day. Every day we're born anew, every moment we're new. There is no such thing as a person in form that doesn't die moment by moment. They are here to be the guidepost, to not let you get stuck, to not let you live in a dead image of self, to not let you fall prey to the fears of others, but to rise and march forward to the fulfillment of your destiny.

While you must set boundaries for YOUR growth, with another adult, you are not the gateway to their growth. They are on their own journey. However, you are a gateway to healing. As you focus on your own journey and removing fear, your influence on their energy is profound. Because you are so connected, every time you heal and recover another aspect of your personality that is frightened, you allow them to do the same.

It is because we live in this illusion that we are separate that we experience fear in the first place. Imagine that this is your reality and every single person in it is playing a role to serve you somehow in your growth. When you die, they all come together, and you realize they are just a part of you that was helping the whole to evolve. I'm not saying this is the case, but it is helpful to look at it in this way. You are the creator. You are the designer. You are the student, and you are the teacher. It is ONLY your evolution that matters! You cannot depend on any other person to do anything for you, be it make you happier or make you miserable. They simply do not have this power. YOU have this power. You alone. If you were to 100% focus on only you and your healing, those around you would match it. In this game of life, some players may exit and new players may enter as you level up. Detach from each individual and know that this is absolutely by design. There is no one you should long for but your whole being. No one. That is the point of this life. For you to step away from fear and journey into a loving, authentic state.

I know this may all sound like bullshit. It may even seem like a foreign language to you. You may not be able to understand it right now, but you will. Every experience that you are having and every person you meet is in your life to somehow play a role in your evolution. How do you know if you're not evolving? If you are stuck. If the people and experiences don't change. If the scenery change but the scenarios don't. If you never seem to up-level. If everyone seems to abandon you. If you can't trust anyone. If it feels like everyone is judging you. All that you need to do to finish this level and move on is to sit down and ask what is here for you: How is this serving me? What are they mirroring for me? What place am I coming from most of the time? What am I afraid of? You must be brutally honest in this process. You may need a coach or trusted mentor to help you bring everything to the light of consciousness.

In the case of a disconnected relationship, the most likely thing they are mirroring for you after you have already spent significant time on the work is a fear that exists solely about the relationship itself. It is a failure to see where you have shut down because you are so resentful and angry with them that you don't even want to look outside of that emotion. Yet staying stuck in this place, even if you move to a state of love and presence most of the time (with this unconscious undercurrent of fear), means that you will not actually be showing them evidence that they are loved, and the relationship will remain stuck.

You are not being asked to give up even more of yourself by giving your husband or wife evidence of your love. On the contrary, you are making the decision TO love yourself. The truth is that you cannot receive what you cannot give. So even if your husband has been showing you that you ARE loved, you have been overlooking it - it hasn't matched your story. It hasn't matched your intention to find evidence that the relationship is over. The love has likely been there, but you have had glasses on that filter it out.

Move Out of Fear

Whatever you believe about yourself is exactly how others will treat you. If you believe that you are hot and sexy, your husband or wife will see you as hot and sexy. If you believe that you are capable and brave, you will accomplish anything you intend to achieve. If you believe that you are a loving wife or husband, you will be. If you believe that you are always abused, you will be. If you believe that you are neglected, you will be. This sounds like some kind of magic, but it's really not. It's how much power you have over your reality.

I read a fascinating story about what the afterlife looks like in a book called *The Ancient Secret of the Flower of Life* by Drunvalo Melchizedek. He writes that when we go out into this formless dimension, we are such powerful creators that whatever we think instantly appears. This is a terrible experience if the person is frightened and they start to recall their fears; snakes, drowning, etc. Whatever they are afraid of is then suddenly instantly in their reality. I imagine this is where the idea of hell came from.

As I've learned more about the kingdom of heaven being something that is actually available to us right now in this lifetime, that it is merely a state of being rather than a place we go when we die, I understand that hell is quite literally somewhere most of us exist in already. We live in such states of fear that our reality matches it—not instantly as in the formless dimension—but quick enough. The universe is always conspiring to show us what we believe.

Because when we are in a state of fear we are looking for someone to fight or flee from, and because we have chosen to marry and live with another, we choose them to blame whether they were the cause of our fear or not. They are guilty by convenience. As our story builds that they are the cause of our fear, we continue to make our relationship the biggest stage for our fear to play out in our reality. We still have unhealed inner child parts that are stuck in fear about something we experienced as young children; parts we need to reach out to and re-parent. As children or experiences touch those old wounds, we are catapulted back into the fearful state. Then we look for someone to blame and point the finger. We then give up our power and pretend we are no longer the designer of our life.

Heal the wounds, acknowledge your role, and commit to a new intention of seeing evidence of their love and making sure they see evidence of yours. Reconnection can happen in one day. You will need to continually check yourself as new stimulus appears that launches you back into a fearful state. You will need to continually remind yourself that you are powerless to change anything about the person in front of you by looking at the person in front of you. You will need to continually remind yourself that your power is in YOUR work, in YOUR beliefs about yourself, and in YOUR commitment to being the fullest expression of you possible.

Marriage is not work. YOU are the work. The marriage will continually reflect your growth back to you, your love for yourself back to you. If it feels like too much work, it is because you have resisted yourself so much that you are exhausted from the energy it takes to deny yourself. When we love ourselves, we love others freely. When we have compassion for ourselves, we have compassion for others. When we acknowledge our own need for growth, we allow them to match it. If it feels like you are there, floating high on your own, and they continually yank you back down to earth, there is something you're still missing, some piece of you that is asking you to look at it and its fear. It's asking you to change your intention for the relationship and your belief about who you are in the context of it.

You are not owned by the relationship. You are the creator of its quality. You are the author of its story. You and you alone.

What You Focus on Grows

Because what we focus on grows, if we decide that our husband is a jerk, that becomes our reality. Remember when you were dating? Nothing could sway your opinion of your lover, because you were only focused on the good.

The key to nearly any achievement you want to have in this life is setting the intention to achieve it. This goes for the next moment, your vacation, your career, and your relationship. If you have the intention that you are going to have a loving experience with your husband, then your actions will reflect it, and your experience will gradually match it. You must first feel the way you WANT to feel all of the time to attract everything in life that matches that frequency.

Our brains want to label everything to make sense of it all, to intellectualize and analyze it so we can make the most efficient choice. That's great if we're choosing between five brands of the same salad dressing, but it doesn't serve us so much in a relationship.

The other day, I noticed that the vet wrote every animal's name in quotation marks; "Lucy," "Max," etc. As I thought about how odd that was, I realized that everything around us is labeled similarly; "pen," "husband," "house," "decoration," "money"… just take a moment to look at something and say its label out loud like that, envisioning the quotes. "Oh, this is a *'PENCIL'*!" It kind of makes you crack up, right?? That's all we've done—we've just assigned everything a label so we can talk about it and communicate. The label itself takes away the magic of the object.

Eckhart Tolle again has a great exercise in his book, *A New Earth*, where he asks that you grab the closest thing to you and just be fully present with it, observing everything about it but labeling nothing at all. Spend five minutes just taking in everything you can about the object. Notice the sensations that you feel, the clarity of vision you suddenly have. When you're fully immersed in observing the object without labels, you are fully present. When I did this with a sparkly, bejeweled bracelet next to me, I suddenly felt exactly like I did when I was a younger child. It was like I was transported in time, instantly a little girl in my bedroom delighting in the way the light danced across glitter.

We recently discovered a mouse in our house. We'd only seen her in brief glimpses as she flew past, but then a few days ago I was in the pantry, and there she was! She seemed to move at warp speed, but I happened to record it on video on my phone, so I was able to go back to her three-second appearance and freeze the frame. She was gray and fluffy with big ears, and I could sense her happy spirit just from the picture.

Of course, if you think of the word "mouse," there are all kinds of associations—disease, bite, filth, sick, nuisance, mess, poop—you get the idea. From that label, then, it's easy to go to my husband's route and get a glue trap. Get rid of it. "You have to catch it and kill it, or it will multiply." I do know that may be true, but when I remove the label and just see the life behind it, I have reverence and respect for it. It's just another being trying to survive, just like me. It's in the wrong place (*or we are*), but that can be fixed. We can try other methods to get them out without going straight to a slow, painful death. I threw out his glue traps and happily tended to humane traps instead. Just because it's a mouse doesn't mean it's less worthy than I am. Isn't this what the famous Aesop's fable, *The Lion and The Mouse*, is about? In it, the lion is awoken by a mouse and lays his paw on her to kill her. She pleads, "Please let me go and some day I will surely repay you." Eventually the tiny mouse does save the mighty lion by chewing through the ropes of a hunter's net that held him. The fable ends, "A kindness is never wasted."

Labels give us license to kill. They give us layers of separation from life itself. Your marriage is one place where you should throw out the labels, spreadsheets, the associations, the statistics, and even the books - just not this one! Pre-conceived ideas do not serve you here. Labeling your husband or wife disallows you to have reverence for the life within them, for the divinity they are just by being energy from the same Source of all life. Not one decision made from the intellect serves the sacred role of relationship, of being in union with another soul who walks upon this earth. Here your brain doesn't help you. It is out of its league. Here, only your heart matters.

If you are present, in only THIS moment, with your spouse, then your heart will guide you. It will commune with the field of energy that connects us all and lead us in the path best for our evolution. It will even cause you to do or not do things that help those in your energy field grow.

If you label your husband as "bad" in any one of its myriad forms, then your brain will get stuck in a loop of all of the associations with that label. The old status quo reaction will be pulled up from your brain's database, and all your mind will do is keep offering you that response, over and over. Check out of your thoughts through meditation and drop into your heart. This situation is without labels. This is your life. Only from an energetic state of love with an empty mind can you clearly see the answer, clearly access the wisdom, and clearly take action—starting with developing your voice to speak what you need.

13 Steps to Begin Reconnecting

I believe these are the steps to foster reconnection in a marriage. Note that these aren't little things like resentfully texting them that they are awesome or that you appreciate them. It's a process where the pre-requisite is that you agree to get to know yourself so deeply that you feel authentically you by the end, that you let nothing come between you and shining your light:

Step One:

Release them from any roles or expectations. Shift the focus to only you.

Step Two:

Commit to stop reacting to their behavior. Start a regular meditation practice.

Step Three:

Commit to re-fueling your own tank every single day. Take ownership of making sure your needs are met. Encourage them to take time, space, and resources to meet their own needs.

Step Four:

Identify your own co-creation, negativity, and subconscious intention for the relationship

Step Five:

Uncover the lessons they are in your life to teach you. Commit to living authentically and walking away from behavior that doesn't reflect your worth. Change patterns.

Step Six:

Energetically thank and release them for the lessons they came into your life to teach you. Let the universe know that the lesson is complete, you get it.

Step Seven:

Identify ANY remaining fear and release it, and commit to raising your vibration to a high-frequency state of love no matter what happens—an easy way to get to this state is gratitude and appreciation.

Step Eight:

Set the intention to stay in a committed and loving relationship with them

Step Nine:

Every day, find evidence that you are loved. Create evidence for your partner that they are loved. You may even keep track of this as a note in your phone for a while.

Step Ten:

Commit to verbally giving them empathy, reminding them that they are capable yet supported, and communicate without judgment, shame, or accusations. Instead, state what you feel and need and then make a specific request for something they can do that would help you.

Step Eleven:

Before all action—eating, cleaning, shopping, how you use your time, etc.—ask yourself what the choice would be that reflects your love for yourself. Let your actions and your environment align with your authenticity.

Step Twelve:

Touch each other daily, in a loving way, seek to exchange love energy. Receive the love you are given without expectation but with reverence & gratitude for the life behind it.

Step Thirteen:

Nurture the relationship as though it were a delicate flower—let it feel life, love, trust, peace, joy, and happiness daily. Delight in their presence every time. When ready, start spending regular time alone together.

Authentic Action Step #11:

Identify your intentions, conscious and subconscious, for this relationship.

Chapter 12: *Your One True Love*

We have covered so much. We have uncovered the truth of what marriage was conceived to be and why that construct no longer serves us. We understand that fear drives relationship trouble and unhealed parts of us continue to be mirrored back to us. We understand now that leaving the person we're in a relationship with often only means that we will continue to receive the same lessons from another.

Now we see that the people in our lives change as we grow, and while early relationships may require us to leave them and move on, the lingering marriage is often a perfect playground for our ascension into higher levels of consciousness.

Now that we are clear on what a relationship is and isn't, what are some ways that you can recommit to your marriage?

First, let's look at the vows we said on our wedding day. Some version of the following was likely uttered if you had a Western marriage:

"I, ____, take you, ____, for my lawful wife/husband, to have and to hold from this day forward, for better, for worse, for richer, for poorer, in sickness and health, until death do us part."

Or

"I, ____, take you, ____, to be my husband/wife. I promise to be true to you in good times and in bad, in sickness and in health. I will love and honor you all the days of my life."

The Lifetime Commitment

So now, I want you to sit down and write two sets of vows. The first will be for a brand new marriage you are about to enter. You are going to marry yourself. Think about what it truly means to love, honor, and cherish yourself. What it means to be responsible for your choices and actions, beliefs and intentions. What does it look like to love yourself? What choices are loving? What does a loving environment look like? What does it mean for you to set boundaries that honor who you are? To respect and have reverence for the life within you? What do you promise yourself from this day forward?

I encourage you to find some symbol of this commitment; it could be jewelry, a tattoo, a painting - whatever you can look at on a daily basis to remind you that first and foremost, you commit to you. You realize that you cannot give others what you do not give yourself. You cannot love your partner until you love yourself. You cannot honor another until you 100% commit to honoring yourself. This is the goal of any relationship. This is what we raise our kids to be capable of and what we must model to them, and it is what our relationships ultimately ask of us in every situation. There is nothing kind you can do for another if you are not doing it for yourself first.

What promise do you make to yourself today that you will honor the rest of your life?

What do you commit to in order to maintain your energy, so you have an abundant overflow from which to give others?

What responsibility do you take for your emotional state or vibrational frequency? In what ways will you raise it?

Give yourself the tangible symbol of this commitment and recite your new vow to yourself, and truly step into and feel your own love, your own role as the embodiment of the Creator of all life, and your intimate connection to and oneness with all of life itself.

The Spiritual Partnership

The second set of vows to write is to your current spouse. However, this time I want you to think of it as a "spiritual partnership" rather than a marriage. No one is possessed, no one is owned, no one has blind commitment to the other, no one is lesser than, no one is setting expectations. This is a partnership created now in the consciousness of free will, recognizing that it may not last a lifetime. Only the marriage to yourself is promised to you for a lifetime. Having and holding this sovereign being may only last until tomorrow.

The definition of partner is a person who takes part in an undertaking with another or others, especially in a business or company with shared risks and profits.

You are partners with this man or woman you have chosen. What is the undertaking? The undertaking is life, for the moment. There are clearly shared risks and profits. The only promise you can make to them is that you will uphold your end. If you think of any great partnership, that is what is happening - each person takes responsibility for their own role. So this means that you promise to be present in the school of life to the best of your ability at every moment. You know that the end goal is evolution, consciousness, enlightenment. You know that every step you take toward this end of the spectrum means that you will more often than not be in a state of joy.

You release them from being responsible in any way for your happiness. You only ask that they hold you accountable for your growth; which they will do naturally by mirroring it.

A very simple vow for a spiritual partnership might look like this:

"I, _____, choose you, _____, to walk beside me in this earthly form as we journey through life together. I promise to love and honor myself, ensure my needs are met, and take responsibility for my energy and emotional state, and hold you accountable for doing the same. I promise to recognize my role in the co-creation of our experience. I promise to be authentic in our journey, speak my truth, and heal any frightened parts of me that you help me to uncover. I promise to love you without expectation, dependence, or control. I promise to not ask you to change who it is you are to make me happy. Together we will experience the joy of being and the sacred nature of caring for ourselves, our children, and our belongings. I delight in hearing you, seeing you, and reflecting your worth with my words and actions."

What else might your vows or other agreements say? What are your priorities at this point in time? Keep in mind that these will change as you grow. How will you manage day-to-day responsibilities? How will you shift your obligations to give your partner focused time and attention? How will you have healthy relationships with your belongings, children, money? Get clear on this in your own mind before you sit down with your spouse and come together on it, should you choose to do so. Remembering that fear and limiting beliefs are present in all areas of our life, what can you work on together?

What level of commitment do you have to this relationship? Do you still commit to staying with them the entire rest of your life? We've discussed how this is an impossible contract, knowing that who you are today is different from who you are tomorrow. How can you re-enter this relationship with commitment but honor the fact that you are always changing?

Commit to only your own growth. Commitment to the relationship is a commitment to your personal growth because the other will continue to mirror your growth back to you. If you commit to your own growth, you ARE committed to them. However, you are not bound to them. Commit to honoring yourself and the other but do not be attached to them. Recognize that there is a natural cycle of life and death on this earth. From the seasons to the menstrual cycle, to the moon -- the way of nature is to have ebbs and flows. Periods of rest and dormancy and periods of high energy and growth.

Therefore, relationships may experience this cycle, or we may experience it throughout our lifetime, with some relationships dying and new relationships forming. If you commit to yourself and set the intention to see evidence of their love for you and yours for them always, allow nature to take the wheel on the length of the relationship. They could die tomorrow. All that matters is that at THIS moment you are committed to this intention. We serve no one when we live in the future, that only serves anxiety. The human form changes and eventually dies and decays. When that happens is out of our control. The love you have for your spouse should be contingent only on this moment, not what could happen in the future or what has happened in the past. In this moment, do you love yourself? In this moment, can they see evidence of your love for them?

There is no vow that you can make outside of this very moment. There is, however, an intention that you can set that you live by. If you are going to share your life with another, you invite them into your life to help you grow. They may decide that they can't, that you have refused to keep growing, or your lack of growth is no longer serving them. If they choose to leave, that is their decision. You can't go through life expecting that they will stay no matter what. You must take personal responsibility for your life and know that whatever happens is a reflection of your willingness to stay the course toward wholeness at all times.

Life isn't so very serious. If it feels that way, you have allowed yourself to become far too bogged down by things. Material possessions are ruling your life. Detach, let go, find alternate ways of living that better support your ability to be unabashedly you. All of these things you acquire for comfort are like the pea under the mattress in the famous fairy tale of the Princess and the Pea. Imagine, everything you own, literally in bed with you at night. Energetically this is what's it like to acquire so many things. You take the energy of them with you wherever you go. If life seems serious, hard, and depressing, there is way too much coming to bed with you every night. Seek to live more simply and to lessen your material possessions as much as you can. Keep what brings you joy and feels light and sacred to take care of. Hoarding resources only serves to weigh down your flow and keep you stuck in a place of anxiety or depression. There is not a single material object that can add or take away from who it is you truly are. Not one belonging is part of you. It is merely baggage you are carrying with you through life. This is the same with food and substances. Whatever you have or do in excess is making your life seem serious. Examine what it costs you to carry the weight of that energetic load. Once you release you allow for more abundance to enter your life. Then life won't seem so overwhelming.

Whatever pulls you out of the present moment: release it.

Whatever pulls you into the past: release it.

Whatever pulls you into the future: release it.

If releasing it means physically giving away or selling a material object, do it. If releasing it means examining fear that is arising for you,

214

then exam it so you can release it. If releasing it means making a phone call to take care of something you have been putting off, make the phone call. Success in this life is not a place you arrive at, it's a series of successful moments. If this moment you are not successful, release it and find what makes it successful. That may mean putting down the phone and connecting with those in your home. It may mean that you stop scrolling Facebook and go do some kind of art or craft that you enjoy.

I read something the other day that said if you aren't creating, you're destroying. Creation is divine, and any time you seek to create, you are in flow. You are putting value out into the world. For me, it may look like writing, and for you, it may look like cooking. Whatever you enjoy creating, do that. That is the doing you are here to do. No matter how much work it feels like, worrying about or grieving over anything is never doing.

Become present. Align. Take Action. Create. The choice is yours how successful you are, how happy you are in this moment, this lifetime.

So, create a vow or intention that you can share with your new spiritual partner (or just keep in mind as your own commitment) that really serves you to understand what this partnership is about and all of the ways it will help you on your journey. Create a partnership that is mutually beneficial, with each partner committing to rediscovering their wholeness and that there is nothing to fix, that each holds all of the answers they need within. Create a partnership that is focused on allowing the other to unfold, without any expectations other than the promise to not disallow this unfolding.

I don't even honestly remember what my marriage vows were. We were married in the courthouse, and I just said: "I do." To say I was ignorant of what marriage really meant is an understatement. It was the fairytale, minus all of the fancy things (and the prince) I had anticipated when I was younger. It was a step toward feeling worthy, not a step made knowing my worth. It was the thrill that someone was committing to me with all of my flaws for the rest of their life. I had no idea about what it would have meant to be fully committed to myself, first. The marriage became part of my sense of self: I am this man's wife. I will add this to my sense of self. This is who I am.

That is bullshit. This marriage has nothing to do with who I am. This man has nothing to do with who I am. This name I took on has nothing to do with who I am. Who I am is divine, perfect, cannot be destroyed, pure love. No one else can change who I am. Had I known my unfathomable worth when I decided I wanted to live with this man, marriage would have been the last thing on my mind. It would have been almost laughable. I wouldn't have felt any insecurity, any doubt, any need, any dependency, or any desire to control my situation.

My path since that time has been one of awakening to this truth of who I authentically am. It has taken me almost four years to fully "get it." To embody it. To live it. I tell you this to ask you to be patient. To remember that life happens at precisely the right moment in time that it is meant to. There is no hurry to divorce your spouse just as there was never any hurry to marry. The only pressure you should put on yourself is to see what this moment is asking of you. If your marriage seems destined to fail, then your intention, though unconscious, is that it fails.

Once you examine your true intentions and beliefs and fears, you have nowhere to go but up. The process of awakening does not usually happen overnight, and especially not in the context of intimate relationships. This relationship is your gift, your greatest earthly teacher. Not the teacher in the familiar sense we have of someone who shows us the lesson, and it's up to us to learn it. This teacher makes us experience the lesson. You can circumvent this by always being curious. Always asking for guidance and help from your nonphysical teachers and guides. You have the power to get assistance with the lessons. Until you recognize these recurring themes in your life and learn, you will continue to experience them.

So thank the person you're with; they are supporting you through your most important work of all. Recommit to yourself and your world will change. Put a picture of yourself up somewhere that you'll see it every morning and on or under it write: "She/He was the creator of her/his life."

Then feel it and live it every day. No one else is designing this experience that you're having but you.

What do you want to feel tomorrow? Make it so, dear friend. Make it so.

Authentic Action Step #12:

Give yourself an always-visible reminder of your love, and commit to never caging your authentic self again.

Fly free, Divine one.

Acknowledgments

To my beautiful children, I can never thank you enough for being the spark that ignited this fire to do better, be better, love better. I will always strive to be my best for you, and I will fail at times, but your spirits are a constant model of what it means to be genuinely authentic which I will use as my guide.

To my brilliant husband, there are no words to adequately express my appreciation for the gifts you've given me. From the mirror you've held to the support you've provided, to the times you've made me laugh, and most importantly, to your commitment to your own consciousness, I thank you, and I believe in you. I love you.

To the great and powerful Dr. Shefali Tsabary, you have remodeled my inner architecture. I am eternally indebted to you for your profound wisdom and courage. On behalf of all of the lives you've touched, thank you for daring to be you.

To Suzi Lula, you are an earth angel, an example in form of divine love. You have taught me that I am worthy of receiving love, especially my own—perhaps the most important lesson of all. Thank you.

To Cori Meadows, thank you for listening to me cry for an entire year!

To Brigid Hopkins, it is because of you that this book exists, thank you for starting us on this journey.

To my family, for making me what I am today, for doing the absolute best you could, and for not passing down all of the pain you endured. I love and cherish all of you.

To Oprah Winfrey, for putting every teacher I've ever needed in my path at the perfect time. We are blessed because of you. Thank you.

To Fred Rogers, for everything.

To all of the beautiful authors who wrote every book that helped me grow and change.

And to all of the beautiful people who took the time to beta-read this book and offer me such amazing guidance and feedback, I can never repay you for helping to make this a quality work that will serve its readers. Especially Georgia Peterson DeClark and Tia Fagan, who each took the time to go through their notes page by page, thank you!!

Appendix

Key Questions Before Marriage:

The following is some food for thought before you decide to marry someone. It is not necessarily to go through with your partner, though you may wish to. And it doesn't necessarily mean you have to agree on everything. It is merely bringing into your awareness the potential for growth you may have and will likely be faced with. Looking at both of your childhoods and understanding both of your parents' patterns should help you to answer all of these.

However, bear in mind that these things will change as you each evolve. This is just a starting point to identify potential future conflicts. **The fact of the matter is that you will attract your vibrational match—a person operating at or below your level of consciousness. They are a mirror of you and your own ability to love yourself.**

1. What were you shown as a child about spending money? What is money to you? What is your goal with it? Does it feel abundant to you?

2. What were you shown as a child about housekeeping? What does it look like and who does it? How do you feel about it now? Do you tend to tidy up after yourself?

3. Kids are extremely hard work and incredibly inconvenient, are you sure you want them, and why? Would you ever punish our children? Were you punished? Who do you feel should sleep if both parents work? How do you feel about changing jobs/schedules to accommodate our children? Did your parents mirror your emotions and show empathy? Did you feel respected and that your needs were met?

4. What tasks do you see yourself performing to maintain our home and belongings? How do you accomplish these? Do you need reminders/lists or will you see what needs to be done and do it? Who did the chores in your home? Were you taught to keep your space tidy?

5. What were you shown about food as a child—was it controlled? Do you know how to cook? Do you like to cook? Who cooked in your family?

6. How do you feel about your job? Where do you see yourself working in five years? Would you be willing to move anywhere for a job change? Do you feel like investing or running your own business? How will you make retirement achievable? What did your parents do for income and how did they feel about it?

7. Describe your daily personal hygiene habits. What were you shown as a child about personal hygiene and the way we take care of ourselves?

8. How does clutter make you feel? Do you consider yourself more of a minimalist or more of a hoarder? How do you like your space to look or feel? How did your home look as a child? What do you

do with paperwork? Do you have any issues donating old belongings?

9. What were you shown about charity as a child? How are you generous? What kinds of things would you like us to do to give back? How do you feel about volunteering?

10. How do you feel about illness? What were you shown about handling illness as a child? Have you ever cleaned up throw-up or poop? What would you do if our child got very sick in the middle of the night, how would you handle it?

11. Are you handy? Do you like to build or fix things? Would you work with our kids on a project that required building something? Who fixed things in your home as a child?

12. What do you like about travel? Where do you consider the best place to go to relax? How often would you want to take trips and what kind of money would you want to spend on them? What were you shown about travel as a child?

13. Do you like crowds and events, loud music or fairs? What is your idea of a fun weekend or evening? What do you see yourself doing with your kids on the weekends? What did you do for fun as a child? What were you shown about spending money on pleasure?

14. How do you feel about exercise? What do you like to do to move your body? How do you feel about being out in nature? What are your favorite outdoor activities? What were you shown about moving your body as a child?

15. Did anyone you know or love have an addiction to anything— food, alcohol, drugs, sex—when you were a child? How did that affect you? Do you feel like you have any addictions?

16. Who do you consult before you make big decisions? How confident do you feel making decisions on your own? What were you shown as a child about making decisions?

17. Did you feel loved as a child? How were you shown that you were loved? Were you shown empathy? Were your emotions mirrored?

18. How did your parents communicate?

References & Recommended Reading

Anodea, J., (2011). Eastern body, western mind: Psychology and the chakra system as a path to the self. Ten Speed Press.

Beckwith, M. B. (2012). 40 day mind fast soul feast: A guide to soul awakening and inner fulfillment. Culver City, CA: Agape Media International.

Berman, L. (2017). Quantum love: Use your body's atomic energy to create the relationship you desire. Hay House Inc.

Carter, & Jay. (2003). Nasty People: How to Stop Being Hurt by them without Stooping to Their Level. McGraw-Hill Pub.

Chapman, G. D., & Summers, A. (2010). The five love languages: How to express heartfelt commitment to your mate. Nashville, TN: LifeWay Press.

Dale, C. (2014). The spiritual power of empathy: Develop your intuitive gifts for compassionate connection.

Hay, L. L. (2012). Heal your body: The mental causes for physical illness and the metaphysical way to overcome them. Carlsbad, CA: Hay House.

Laozi, & Mitchell, S. (2015). Tao te Ching.

Linn, D., Merlington, L., & Tantor Media. (2018). Sacred Space: Clearing and enhancing the energy of your home. Old Saybrook, CT: Tantor Media.

Lipton, B. H. (2016). The biology of belief: Unleashing the power of consciousness, matter & miracles.

Lula, S., Tsabary, S., & Beckworth, M. B. (2016). The motherhood evolution: How thriving mothers raise thriving children.

Melchizedek, D. (2000). The Ancient Secret of the Flower of Life.

Mitchell, S. (1991). The Gospel according to Jesus. New York, NY: Harper Collins Publishers.

Money, J. (1993). Lovemaps: Clinical concepts of sexual-erotic health and pathology, paraphilia, and gender transposition in childhood, adolescence, and maturity. New York: Irvington.

Moorjani, A. (2015). Dying to be me: My journey from cancer, to near death, to true healing.

Rosenberg, M. B., & Gandhi, A. (2015). Non-violent communication: A language of life. Encinitas, CA: PuddleDancer Press.

Singer, M. A. (2013). The untethered soul: The journey beyond yourself.

Tolle, E. (2008). A New Earth: Awakening to your life's purpose. New York: Penguin.

Tsabary, S. (2015). The conscious parent: Transforming ourselves, empowering our children. Grand Haven, MI: Namaste Publishing/Brilliance Audio.

Tsabary, S. (2016). The awakened family: A revolution in parenting.

Vanzant, I. Y. (2017). TRUST: Mastering the four essential trusts: Smiley Books.

Weiss, B. L. (2012). Many lives, many masters: The true story of a prominent psychiatrist, his young patient, and the past-life therapy that changed both their lives.

Winfrey, O., & Robbins, A. (2017). The Wisdom of Sundays.

Zukav, G., Winfrey, O., & Angelou, M. (2016). The seat of the soul. New York: Simon and Schuster.

ADHD and Dopamine: What's the Connection? (n.d.). Retrieved from https://www.healthline.com/health/adhd/adhd-dopamine

Chapter 06: Energetic Communication - HeartMath Institute. (n.d.). Retrieved from https://www.heartmath.org/research/science-of-the-heart/energetic-communication/

Edward Jay Epstein. (n.d.). Have You Ever Tried to Sell a Diamond? Retrieved from https://www.theatlantic.com/magazine/archive/1982/02/have-you-ever-tried-to-sell-a-diamond/304575/

The Energetic Heart Is Unfolding - HeartMath Institute. (2015, March 25). Retrieved from https://www.heartmath.org/articles-of-the-heart/science-of-the-heart/the-energetic-heart-is-unfolding/

Harvard Health Publishing. (2015, May 20). How addiction hijacks the brain - Harvard Health. Retrieved from https://www.health.harvard.edu/newsletter_article/how-addiction-hijacks-the-brain

Noah Feldman. Cherokees' Gay-Marriage Law Is Traditional (2015, December 14). Retrieved from https://www.bloomberg.com/view/articles/2016-12-14/cherokees-gay-marriage-law-is-traditional

William Doherty: How Therapy Can be Hazardous to Your Marital Health. (n.d.). Retrieved from http://www.smartmarriages.com/hazardous.html

The Memory of Love...

October 18th, 2018: A friend invites me to see the movie, *A Star is Born*, with Lady Gaga and Bradley Cooper. I'm sitting in the dark theater, loving all of the messages about being authentic and finding your voice, when Bradley's character, who's riding a motorcycle, reaches down behind him and touches Gaga's leg. Hot tears begin to flood my eyes.

Instantly I'm back in 2008, remembering the feel of a loving hand on my own leg, rapid imagery of the juicy love I used to share with my husband flashing through my mind. The tears don't stop for hours. Something new inside opens as they fall.

Our story? To be continued...

Thank You!

Thank you from the bottom of my heart for journeying with me. Please reach out and share your story! Visit bethrowles.com.

XO,

Beth

Some Fun Facts:

… *Three* diamonds fell out of my wedding ring during the writing of this book.

… The cover art is a painting I did in one day, sometime around 2012, before this journey began. I was mortified by it and shoved it in the back of a closet. I found it during writing and realized it was pretty much every concept in this book, in one painting.

Thank You!

Made in the USA
Columbia, SC
13 March 2020